THE ULTIMATE ACT OF

being
enough

Leisa WALLACE

Memoir Disclaimer: This work is a memoir. Names, identifying details, locations, and personal characteristics have been changed to protect the privacy of others. Dialogue is reconstructed from memory, and some events may be compressed or re-ordered for narrative flow.

First Edition
Hardcover: 979-8-9936834-0-9
Audiobook: 979-8-9936834-1-6
Paperback: 979-8-9936834-2-3
Ebook: 979-8-9936834-3-0

Cover Design, Interior and Audiobook Narration by Leisa Wallace

Contents

To Mom

For teaching me I'm a divine being,
not a divine doing.

Introduction

You were doing everything right—until suddenly, you couldn't. The stopping wasn't a choice; it was an ambush. One moment, you were ticking off the last item on your to-do list. Next, everything simply ceased.

The future blurred. The normal you knew vanished. And in that sudden, unasked-for stillness, a scream echoed: "If I can't do, who am I?"

For me, the silence that followed was a vacuum—cold and terrifying—where my identity once resided. My body, once a finely tuned machine, now felt like a lead weight. Every movement reminded me I was no longer working the way I used to. Worse—I *could* no longer work the way I used to.

Not just professionally, but in the tiny, absurd, everyday ways. I'd forget my own email password mid-login. I'd try to make dinner and end up crying on the kitchen floor. Folding laundry felt like an Olympic sport. I once took a nap after brushing my teeth.

My brain was still running at a hundred tabs open, but my body had shut down the whole browser.

Here's the unsettling truth nobody tells us: most of us grew up inside a paradox. I call it the Worth Paradox. Two truths, both deeply ingrained, both treasured—yet fundamentally at odds. The first truth: work hard, serve others, and strive for excellence. Do it all, and do it flawlessly.

I lived this truth with the precision of a color-coded calendar. I ran committees, met deadlines, taught classes, remembered birthdays, and sent late-night texts while the rest of the world slept. I didn't believe in just doing—I believed in doing it all, doing it flawlessly, and then doing more. Always more.

I spent vacation days building someone else's dream and rest days answering messages that couldn't wait. I told myself I was being faithful when, really, I was afraid of being forgotten. Hustle didn't feel optional; it felt sacred—because action promised acceptance. Hustle offered belonging. Work equaled worth.

And there was a thrill to it—the electric buzz of urgency, caffeine, and deadlines humming through my veins. The tap of keys became percussion, my heartbeat syncing to the tempo of output. Each "well done" was a spark that kept the engine burning. I told myself it was purpose. In truth, it was dopamine dressed up as devotion.

The second truth was a beautiful, distant echo. You are a divine being. Created with purpose. Loved eternally. Endowed with worth beyond measure.

I believed it—on paper. But when life slammed me against the wall and stripped away everything I could do, that belief collapsed under its own weight.

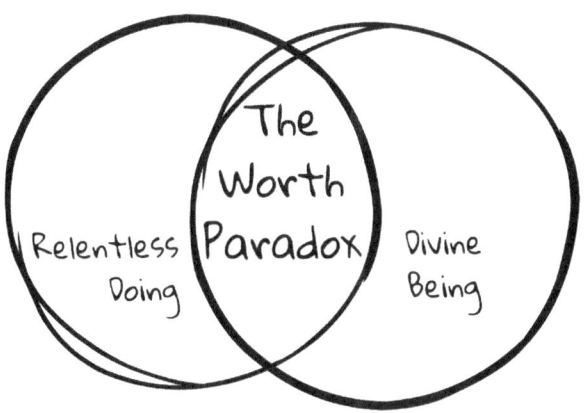

The collision of two sacred truths:
our drive to prove, and our divine assurance that we never needed to.

How could I be divine when I couldn't even get out of bed? How could I have purpose when I couldn't contribute? How could I possess worth when I had nothing left to give?

It's this contradiction in the Worth Paradox that unraveled me—and perhaps this incongruity resonates for you too. Because this isn't just my story; it's a societal epidemic.

In a world wired for performance—where we collect followers, track sleep, gamify meditation, and quantify every breath—our worth has become data-driven. And in the quiet, we're all asking: who am I when I'm not producing?

I wasn't wrestling with doubt. I was grappling with dissonance. That ache—a constant thrum beneath my skin—demanded an answer.

So, I went searching—not for a cure for my body, but for a way to rebuild my soul. I chased answers across disciplines: theology, psychology, trauma recovery, and even leadership and business frameworks. (Hustle, it turns out, is everywhere.)

But chronic illness forced a kind of integration most people never experience, where theory had to become a lifeline and ideas had to hold.

I wasn't hunting for a perfect fix, but for something sturdy enough to hold both truths—something steady enough to hold me.

Piece by piece, a new logic emerged, shattering everything I thought I knew about value.

What I found wasn't a formula or a comeback plan. What I found was a Constellation Map—a guide to tracing the scattered, enduring lights of my intrinsic strengths, those unmeasured elements that survive when achievement fails. This pattern of meaning had been shining all along, waiting for me to notice.

That's what this book offers. Not a five-step strategy or a bounce-back blueprint, but the guide I desperately needed when I felt lost.

It's a way through collapse, grief, and disorientation—leading you toward something profoundly stronger than striving: a quiet power, an unshakable peace, a steady Core no crisis can weaken.

A reminder that your Light hasn't faded. And your worth was never something you had to earn.

Did it erase the pain? No. But it gave me words. Words that helped me stop striving to get back to who I thought I was and begin discovering who I already am. Words that helped me redefine a good life—not by output, but by alignment. And those words illuminated a path forward.

I didn't have to become someone else. I just had to remember who I'd been all along.

If you've ever sat in the quiet after collapse, wondering who's left when the doing stops, this is for you. You don't have to walk this alone.

This is the map I built back to myself—a Constellation Map—a way to trace the scattered Lights of who I'd always been and to find the profound peace that comes from living from your Core.

And now it's yours. Because your worth was never something you had to earn. It was always meant to be remembered, reclaimed, and realized.

Unravel

Part One

When Life Falls Apart,
Your Worth Starts to Surface.

Chapter 1

Unravel

Sometimes the Fall Is the First Mercy

Measured but Not Seen

The cold MRI table pressed against my spine, draining the last warmth from my body. Each shallow breath carried metallic fear. My muscles tensed, but I stayed still, unwilling to disrupt the scan. The room pulsed with the machine's rhythm, its mechanical noises drowning everything but my heartbeat.

Even my raw existence was reduced to a series of data points. The monitor's steady beeping echoed through the tunnel, each ping a brutal measure: heart rate 72, oxygen saturation 98%, respiratory rate 16. Numbers that confirmed I was alive but whispered nothing about whether I was okay. It struck me even then how easily we let ourselves be flattened into what can be quantified, silencing the deeper, unmeasurable truths of our experience.

The sterile tunnel narrowed, harsh clinical Lights pressing in. The air smelled of antiseptic and static—clean, but not comforting. Claustrophobia pressed in from all sides; the sense of being trapped went beyond the physical.

Stillness was my only survival, yet it became an unforgiving mirror, reflecting all my strongest reactions. What couldn't be captured in a chart—my fear, my grief, my deepest fire—began to scream for acknowledgment.

This wasn't just a scan; this was a reckoning. A raw initiation into a truth we all face: the familiar crumbles, and we're left to wonder where meaning lives when it can't be found in the data.

The Efficiency Trap

Looking back, I call this the Efficiency Trap—the belief that if I could control, optimize, measure, and receive validation, I'd finally be safe. But this thinking is cruel; metrics could never hold my soul.

The magnets inside the machine whirred to life, their energy vibrating around my skull in an invasive, almost aggressive way. The low, continuous hum—interrupted by sharp clanking—was less a sound and more a violation of the silence. It circled my head like it knew me, like it had been waiting for this moment to dissect everything I was trying to hold together. Not just searching for illness, but for the cracks in my identity.

This was more than a diagnosis. It felt like exposure. I realized, in that moment, that the doctors suspected something so deeply wrong that it had to be uncovered and fixed.

And what if the data found what even I had been unwilling to name?

The ER doctors were blunt, their words clinical and detached, offering no solace as they spoke of tests and uncertainty. But their eyes—their eyes screamed volumes, already anticipating answers that would forever alter my life: something neurological, something permanent.

Their restrained distance echoed, a chasm between their expertise and my unraveling. It's in these moments of profound uncertainty that we confront the limits of external validation. No amount of expertise can truly convey the human experience of losing control.

The MRI scan wasn't just a checkup. It was the beginning of a new chapter I wasn't ready to write. As I lay there, motionless, waiting for the machine to finish its work, the fear—that looming dread—sank deeper. Something was being uncovered. I had no idea what, but the truth would soon be revealed.

Just hours earlier, I'd been in my elementary school classroom—my haven, my place of control. A space where I'd always felt grounded, perfectly balanced between teaching and motherhood. The day had hummed with its usual rhythm: children's chatter, lessons unfolding, and a dozen plans in motion.

And me? I was at my best—organized, precise, in charge. I didn't just thrive on it; I needed it. It was more than a job. It proved I mattered.

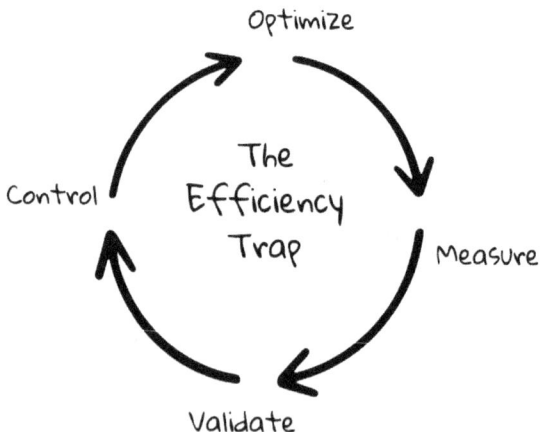

When perfomance becomes proof of worth, the cycle never ends.

That morning, my hands moved with breathless efficiency—snapping a laminated schedule to the whiteboard, answering a parent's email with one hand while setting out math manipulatives with the other. I'd nod at coworkers, zip a lunchbox shut, adjust a child's glasses, and redirect a squabble over markers—all before the bell rang. The kids didn't notice, but I did. Every task clicked into place. I was spinning twelve plates, not a single one wavering. This was my rhythm, my proof, my power.

Perfection wasn't a performance. It was my peace.

There was a sacred safety in knowing the plan and executing it flawlessly. The satisfaction of a perfectly submitted report, of a child's achievement feeling like my own success, was the currency of my worth. If everything ran smoothly, I was enough.

Even then, part of me knew the value wasn't in the test scores. It was in the sparkle of understanding when a student finally got it. But that part had been buried—beneath the metrics, beneath the pressure, and beneath the need to always do more.

The only anomaly had been a slight tingling in my feet, a sensation I'd briskly dismissed as a pinched nerve—nothing more.

But as the hours passed, that tingling deepened, creeping, relentless. I could feel it moving through me, slowly, an insidious tide that refused to recede. What began as minor discomfort intensified, an invisible weight pressing down on my limbs. By the time the bell rang and the children scattered, the numbness had spread further, snaking into my arms and fingers. My hands, usually so confident with markers, zippers, and lunchbox lids, now fumbled—alien, as if they no longer belonged to me. It wasn't just physical anymore. My body, once a loyal instrument, was turning on me: a silent, terrifying rebellion in every nerve.

By evening, swallowing felt like grit; each sip of water or bite of food was a monumental, gasping task. My steps, once brisk and assured, now felt like a toddler's first attempts—uncertain, unstable, agonizingly slow. My throat locked, as if I'd swallowed glass. I pressed a palm to my chest, but the panic pulsed underneath, sharp and unrelenting—coiled in my ribs like a predatory second heartbeat.

What had seemed like a minor worry at breakfast had transformed into something undeniable, inescapable. The emergency room visit wasn't an overreaction anymore—it was my lifeline. Hours had shifted everything. What had once been normal, mundane, now seemed distant, a fading memory. The reality of my situation was becoming clear: something was wrong.

The world, hours ago a familiar map, had dissolved beneath me. Confined within this chamber, the MRI's hum vibrated through me, reducing me to images and data points. Every shift of the machine seemed to strip away my identity, preparing me to be plotted and analyzed. Doctors would use those markers to determine my fate.

But as I lay motionless, unable to move, a thought sparked within me—a small, defiant flicker. Was I truly just a set of measurements? Was my entire existence to be reduced to these cold, clinical outputs?

What the Numbers Can't Hold

"Numbers tell stories," I'd told my students countless times. Numbers could quantify, measure, and explain, yes, but they also held deeper meaning. Now, those words echoed, a cruel irony, mocking me as I lay on that table, reduced to mere digits on a screen.

Data couldn't capture the essence of who I was—my pain, my fear, my resilience. It couldn't understand the fight I was about to face. And yet, here I was: a set of readings awaiting interpretation. A soul beneath statistics. A life awaiting a label.

But that deep part of me—the one protesting reduction—wasn't just poetic longing. It was something psychologists have long affirmed. Studies by Deci and Ryan show that human beings are wired for intrinsic motivation—for meaning that springs not from external rewards, titles, or outcomes, but from autonomy, connection, and a sense of purpose. When our worth is tied to metrics, we may perform, but we do not thrive.

This was more than a medical scan—it was an existential one. In that moment, I saw that my challenge was not just about receiving a diagnosis. It was about confronting the central truth: my worth and identity could not be minimized to performance or measurement, no matter how much I craved control. Rediscovering meaning beyond numbers became the real lesson.

When was the last time you felt degraded to a title, a role, or a result? What parts of you can't be charted but still shape how you love, lead, or serve? If everything paused right now, what story would the silence tell? And perhaps even more importantly: how do we help others feel seen when the world renders them invisible?

The technician's voice crackled through the speaker, its detached command shattering my train of thought. "Try to stay completely still. This sequence will take about seven minutes."

Seven minutes. The number clung to me, a desperate mantra. I had to endure and breathe, every part of me now in the hands of this machine. That number, heavy as a stone, pressed down. It wasn't just time; it represented the vast unknown ahead, the churning uncertainty, the raw fear. I couldn't help but wonder: if I'm only numbers now, what becomes of everything else?

The truth would soon be revealed. I was not broken. I was being refined. The failure of data allowed something deeper, my authentic self, to speak.

Being Enough

Allowing yourself to grieve the life you planned without rushing to rebuild.

Letting go of worth measured by efficiency, output, or performance.

Trusting that who you are remains when roles collapse and metrics fall silent.

Chapter 2

Collapse

When Identity Breaks, Something Deeper Begins

Identity Quake

F or those of us who forge identity through doing, through mission, and through movement, collapse feels like more than a setback. It's an identity quake.

Sometimes, it's not failure that shakes you—it's success, brutally interrupted.

It cracks the foundation, not just of what you do, but of who you fundamentally are. And yet, in that fracturing, something deeper stirs: a question, a whisper, a beginning you never asked for.

I wasn't just facing a diagnosis; I was losing access to my own body, and with it, the very clarity of who I believed myself to be. This kind of disorientation cuts far deeper than fear. It threatens the entire story of who you are.

And when that story shatters, silence rushes in to take its place.

That silence is terrifying. It's also where the deeper part of you finally begins to speak.

Out of the corner of my eye, I watched our small-town neurologist pace the dimly lit hall. His hurried steps betrayed the late hour and the palpable gravity of the news he carried. Fluorescent Lights cast a cold, clinical glow on his wrinkled lab coat and tired eyes. He moved with practiced purpose, but a stiffness clung to his stride—each step a breath held too long. He looked like a man about to deliver a death sentence, albeit a quiet one.

I was wheeled toward a hospital room, the harsh clatter of the wheels echoing off the tile, jarring in its rhythm. Uncertainty swirled like a storm, and I forced my gaze onto the grout lines beneath me, counting them like a desperate tether to normality. My breath became the only thing I could control. Beneath the numbers, beneath the fear, something else pulsed: a slow, dawning realization that this moment might be asking more of me than simple survival. That something was being stripped away, yes, but what if something wasn't merely being confiscated, but revealed?

Then the wheels stopped. The abrupt stillness hit harder than any motion. It stretched—thick, breathless—just long enough for the dread to fully settle behind my ribs.

"Can you lift your right foot?" The neurologist's voice was gentle, insistent, as if I should be able to do it without question. I stared at my foot, willing it, pleading with it to move, to respond the way it always had. Nothing.

"How about your toes?"

Still nothing.

A strange, unfamiliar immobility settled in. My foot was undeniably part of me, yet it felt distant, foreign. It no longer belonged. The dead weight of my unresponsive limbs grew heavier, crushing my sense of control. It wasn't just the absence of movement—it was the profound hush that accompanied it. My mind screamed for action, but my body refused.

The neurologist turned the glowing screen toward me. Seventeen lesions on my brain. Four on my spine. Unwelcome markers of a new, terrifying reality.

"Aggressive-onset multiple sclerosis," he said.

The words didn't just hit; they splintered my world like a slab of ice.

He rattled off statistics, progression rates, and treatment plans, but I couldn't absorb a single word. Each syllable chipped away at the edges of my identity, replacing the woman I knew with a diagnosis I couldn't comprehend.

The Collapse of the Self

This is the collapse no one talks about: The moment you lose the version of yourself you've spent years cultivating.

For leaders, educators, creatives—anyone driven by mission—this kind of disorientation cuts far deeper than fear; it threatens the entire story of who you are.

I pictured my whiteboard, still half-covered in student handwriting from that morning. My son's hand in mine as we crossed the street. But the images were already faded—washed out, like old photographs left too long in the sun.

It wasn't just my health at stake.

It was my leadership. My motherhood. My movement. My very meaning.

This kind of collapse isn't just physical—it's existential. Psychologist Carl Rogers described becoming a person as a lifelong process of discovering the self beneath all the roles we've been trained to perform. And trauma expert Peter Levine reminds us that when the body is overwhelmed, it speaks through silence, stillness, and sensation—often long before the mind can make sense of what's been lost.

My limbs were quiet. But something inside me had started to scream.

The meticulously built scaffolding of my life—lesson plans, dinner schedules, calendars, color-coded everything—didn't just collapse. It imploded. And as it imploded, I heard an unfamiliar soundlessness beneath the wreckage. Fragments of a forgotten constellation shimmered. Pieces of a story I hadn't yet learned to see. Not absence. Not numbness. This was something more alive, more ancient.

A voice that didn't ask, "Who are you now?" But whispered, "Who were you before all this?"

I wasn't just losing control of my left foot. I was losing the parent-teacher conference I'd promised my son I'd attend, losing the fall hiking trip we'd mapped out in red pen on the calendar, losing the quiet certainty of standing in front of a classroom, of moving freely through my life, of waking up without wondering what I'd lose next.

It wasn't a single event. It was every forward motion I'd built my life around—stalled, frozen, slipping, all at once, out of reach.

The hospital room, once a place where answers were sought, now felt like a sterile cage. The fluorescent Lights hummed overhead, utterly indifferent. The air smelled sharp with antiseptic. Despite the doctor's measured calm, I felt myself shrinking into a chart, a list of stats, a case file in motion.

These new labels circled in my mind, mocking every hard-won title I'd earned:

Teacher → Patient

Mother → Dependent

Independent Spirit → Case File

Future → Unknown

And yet, even in that devastating loss, there was a pause. A sudden, potent space. A choice. This is where the deeper work truly begins—not with clarity, but with the courage to simply listen. Not with answers, but with raw, unwavering presence.

Being Enough

Allowing your worth to exist beyond roles, titles, and labels.

Listening for the self beneath performance and productivity.

Finding presence even in the quiet of collapse.

Chapter 3

See

Being Witnessed is the Beginning of Healing.

Transformation, Not Information

In moments of disorientation—through illness, failure, transition, or unexpected change—we often encounter guides who don't just offer information. They offer transformation. Through them, we often learn to see ourselves in a new Light.

In one of my lowest moments, I met such a guide. Through him, I came to understand something I'd spent my entire professional life resisting:

Sometimes, the numbers lie. They tell us where to look, but rarely what matters most.

Two days blurred into one in the relentless fluorescent haze. I was a patient now—reduced to a mere collection of vitals, a body awaiting assessment. Heart rate, blood pressure, temperature. Each number tracked a shift within me, blinking across monitors with dispassionate clarity. But none of it told my story. No chart captured the ache of invisibility as nurses passed without meeting my eyes, and no line graph conveyed the raw panic that surged at 3 a.m. The numbers were real, but they were hollow, empty without context.

They offered a summary of function, never a reflection of experience. For someone like me—who'd always measured worth by tasks completed, by problems solved—this helplessness was almost harder to bear than the diagnosis itself. I'd spent my life mastering plans, believing preparation could outmaneuver any disaster. No plan, however meticulous, could have prepared me for this.

A Different Kind of Medicine

That evening, when I least expected it, Dave, the hospital pharmacist, arrived. Dressed in a crisp white shirt and tie, he looked jarringly out of place in the impersonal, antiseptic gloom. But his smile—warm, open, and startlingly human—cut through the inhospitable air like pure sun-

Light. In that instant, I wasn't just a patient in a bed; I was a person again.

I expected him to review medications or check dosages—the usual clinical routine. Instead, he pulled up a chair, sat down beside me, and looked me directly in the eye. No iPad, no rush, just an unwavering presence. This wasn't mere bedside manner. It was something deeper. The kind of presence that transforms a moment, a meeting, a life.

"I've had MS for twenty years," he said, his voice calm and steady, as if gently placing a hand on the moment. There was no pity in his words, only Light. "I want to explain more fully what you're going through."

His presence shifted something in me. It wasn't just that he understood the condition theoretically; he understood the human experience of it. And in that understanding, something softened within me. A sense of being witnessed. A tiny opening toward wholeness.

Dave wasn't just offering advice—he was modeling what real leadership under adversity looks like, the kind every purpose-driven professional will one day be called to practice.

He didn't fix me, and he didn't change my condition. But as he sat beside me, truly seeing me, he gave me something no plan ever could: the permission to simply be.

Like the quiet glow of shared starlight—constant, steady, quietly illuminating the dark.

Even his slight strain as he shifted in the chair spoke volumes. He wasn't here just to do a job. He was living this story too.

He was a leader not by title, but by presence. Not because he had answers, but because he embodied them.

He reached into his bag, carefully unfolded a set of diagrams, and laid them on the tray beside my bed.

"Let me show you what's happening to your body," he said, his finger tracing the printed nerve lines on the page. His words were clear and scientific, but his tone was gentle—as if he knew I desperately needed more than information. I needed a way to make sense of things.

"This is how multiple sclerosis affects your nerves," he explained. "It's why you're losing feeling so quickly."

He tapped the diagram again. "Think of your nerves like electrical wires. They're wrapped in insulation—myelin—that keeps the current running cleanly. With MS, your immune system attacks the myelin sheath, the insulation that surrounds nerve cells. Without it, the signals flicker and misfire. Sometimes they travel too slowly, sometimes they cut out altogether. Other times they arrive twisted, like a text message scrambled into nonsense."

Then he showed me my MRI. The lesions stood out—white smudges against a dark backdrop. I followed his finger, each spot a stark, callous reminder of what was happening beneath my skin.

He pointed to the cluster along my spine. "These are why your hands went numb. Your spinal cord is like a central highway, carrying every message from the brain out to the body. When a lesion scars that road, the signal doesn't just slow—it cuts in and out like a bad radio station signal. Sometimes you catch enough of the music to recognize the song. Other times it's only static.

"The hardest part is, MS isn't only about the scars themselves. It's about how your nervous system is functioning around them at any given moment. Think of it like a frayed wire—on some days, the current finds just enough copper to flow. You can walk, you can grip, and you almost forget anything is wrong. But add inflammation, heat, or exhaustion, and that same wire sputters out. The current can't make the jump, and you're left in the dark."

I let him guide me, desperately needing someone else to hold the map. His clarity began to steady me. The chaos inside me began to form a pattern. I could finally see it now—not just the condition, but the story behind it.

And then, just as gently, he added, "The physical recovery will take time. But the emotional recovery is just as important."

That was the first time anyone acknowledged my heart, not just my nerves.

He spoke of therapy: not just physical, but emotional, mental, and spiritual. As he spoke, I realized this wasn't just about walking again. This was about rebuilding my entire life.

Those vital signs the medical staff kept charting never revealed this deeper part of the journey—the part that required courage, grief, unwavering presence, and a fierce will to keep living when you no longer recognized the life you had planned.

This was the moment I understood:

Leadership isn't just about having power. It's about extending presence.

He answered questions I didn't know I had. He gave names to fears I hadn't dared speak aloud. And in doing so, he returned to me something I didn't even realize I'd lost: agency, belonging, the profound sense that I could still shape my own story.

As he stood to leave, something in the room felt fundamentally changed. Not Lighter, perhaps, but undeniably clearer.

And then, with one last, lingering look, he uttered the sentence I will never forget.

"I can't feel my feet. But life is good."

At first, the words seemed simple, almost casual. But they carried a weight I didn't recognize until much later. They weren't about symptoms. They were about soul.

He wasn't merely surviving in spite of MS. He was thriving on purpose. His life wasn't defined by a diagnosis. And in watching him, I began to believe mine didn't have to be either.

The Measure that Matters

The door clicked softly shut behind him. Silence settled over the room. But it was a different kind of silence now—one that held a flicker of Light. A potent seed of belief.

The belief that perhaps presence—not performance—was the truest measure of strength.

That maybe healing began not when everything was fixed, but when you were finally seen.

And for the first time, I began to question the kind of leader I had always been. Until now, leadership had meant action—solving problems, organizing people, meeting goals. But Dave showed me something quieter, and infinitely deeper. His presence didn't demand control; it offered connection. He modeled a leadership rooted not in performance, but in groundedness. Not in answers, but in witness.

He didn't teach me anything new. He helped me remember something profound I had forgotten: that real influence begins with being anchored, authentic, and available. Even in stillness. Even in uncertainty. Especially then.

True leadership isn't about certainty or perfection. It's about carrying hope into uncertain spaces.

And in the unshakeable presence of someone who had already walked that road, I believed it.

But belief was just the beginning. Learning to lead this way myself—without control, without clarity—would take time. I didn't know it yet, but this moment would become the blueprint for rebuilding everything.

Being Enough

Letting presence carry more weight than performance.

Trusting that leadership begins with being, not doing.

Believing life can be good even when it isn't easy.

Chapter 4

Grieve

Letting Go is Sacred. So is What Stays

Unearning

We are relentlessly taught to equate value with output—in our work, our parenting, and our leadership. But what happens when your body stops cooperating, when your energy, stamina, and ability to simply show up vanish? This is when true value isn't earned but uncovered. Like a fossil slowly unearthed, not through force but by quiet patience.

The summer of 2019 stretched before me like an endless desert, each day a peculiar, agonizing mix of monotony and disorienting transformation. Time lost its familiar rhythm. Hours compressed into sharp, searing moments of frustration, then expanded into endless, suffocating periods of waiting, with the quiet ticking of a clock as the only constant sound. SunLight streaming through my bedroom window marked the passage of days, but my internal clock had utterly lost its bearings.

Even my body felt unknowable, shifting constantly beneath me like dry sand.

I tracked small victories: a flicker of sensation in my legs, fleeting warmth in my fingers. These moments proved erratic, painful reminders of MS's relentless attack. Simple movements—reaching for a mug, typing, turning a page—now took careful, exhausting calculation. My body felt less like my will's extension and more like a reluctant, often defiant, ally.

Some mornings, I woke with a desperate sliver of hope. But by afternoon, my limbs often revoked their cooperation entirely. The sheer unpredictability wore at my spirit more profoundly than the pain itself. Each day brought its own fresh puzzle of ability and restriction, a constant, exhausting recalibration of what was possible.

Learning to Listen

I mourned this betrayal in bitter, quiet moments, feeling trapped in a body that defied me. The mirror reflected

someone I struggled to know—not just in appearance
but in my halting, uncertain movements. Some days,
hope glimmered, like sunlight after a storm. These faint
moments kept me moving forward, though were never
quite enough to erase uncertainty's shadows.

With each week, one truth crystallized with devastating clarity: the damage was permanent.

This wasn't a temporary setback or a challenge to overcome through determination.

It was my new reality, as fixed as the gravity that held me
in my chair. Yet within this painful understanding, I began
to glimpse an unspoken, insistent question. Could I live,

not in spite of this body, but in rhythm with it? Could I stop fighting and begin listening?

As I mentioned earlier in this book in the section entitled "Collapse," psychologist Carl Rogers said healing begins when we stop trying to live up to an image and instead embrace who we are. He called this becoming a person—a slow unfolding of the self beneath performance, perfection, and pretense. And again, trauma expert Peter Levine teaches that grief is not just an emotional response; it is a biological response. The body remembers what the mind avoids. Sometimes, only stillness lets us release what was never ours to hold.

And so I began to ask myself quietly: What planned version of my life have I been fighting to preserve—even after it's slipped away?

What would happen if I stopped trying to prove I was still "enough" and simply believed that I already was?

The words of the hospital pharmacist, Dave, became a haunting, persistent echo. "Life is good," he'd said, even without feeling in his feet. He had shown me that worth wasn't tied to what your body could do, but to who you were. A precious seed of hope had been planted, a new way of seeing myself that felt like starLight piercing the clinical darkness. But accepting it intellectually was one thing; truly living it, unlearning decades of tying my value to performance, was another battle.

Reaching for Control

Still, something shifted. Quietly, almost imperceptibly, I began to pause. When the compulsive urge to mentally revamp my classroom hit me—the color-coded bins, the lesson outlines, the perfect transitions—I actively caught myself. Not to stop planning entirely, but to ask, "What would bring peace, not just control?" Sometimes I still defaulted to fixing. But other times, I consciously let the dishes sit. I looked my son in the eye instead of checking my planner. These weren't conscious decisions; they were instincts. My body—and perhaps my soul—was reaching for a softer way of being. Not surrender, but pliability. Not defeat, but presence.

My default setting wasn't harmony; it was rigid control. Even as I sat in my ergonomic desk chair, I found myself mentally rearranging the classroom bins I could no longer lift—desperate to feel useful, to do something. Despite Dave's wisdom, my deepest instinct was still to fight this new reality, to cling desperately to the familiar.

This endless quest for "normalcy" was primal—a belief that my worth was tied to output and performance, a lie many leaders endorse.

As the summer turned to fall, I clung to a single, desperate mantra: if I could just return to the classroom, pull out the lesson plans, and rebuild the routines that had once kept me steady, surely everything would fall into place. I told myself, "I just need to try." But even as I uttered the words, I wasn't sure I believed them. Part of me knew—with aching, quiet certainty—that the person I was trying to reclaim might no longer exist. Still, I reached for the old rhythms like a child reaching for a vanished lullaby. The hope wasn't logical. It was pure longing.

And so I tried. I recreated my so-called masterpiece of efficiency—perfectly labeled bins, precise schedules, the classroom hum that once felt like music. I craved the comfort of perfect rows, the structure that always gave me a sense of control. But reality didn't cooperate. My energy flickered, sputtered, and failed. Standing to teach felt like standing on shattered glass, each moment a fragile test of how long I could hold before breaking. Writing on the board, once automatic, became a slow, shaky negotiation between a desperate mind and uncooperative muscles. The color-coded plans that had once reassured me now mocked me, their clean lines a painful, infuriating contrast to the chaos inside. Every attempt at "normal" drained me—not just physically, but to my very soul.

I was grieving more than a job. I was grieving the effortless confidence, the quick thinking, and the spontaneous joy of a classroom that once felt like an extension of my body and mind. And in my desperate effort to reclaim control, I discovered a far deeper cost. I was losing myself in the relentless striving.

This wasn't just an adjustment. It was a funeral for the life I had planned, and no one had told me how to mourn that.

It was an intense lesson in letting go of who I thought I had to be, to discover who I was.

I had just begun exploring this question when the world itself violently shifted. In March 2020, COVID-19 surged into our lives, layering global anxiety on top of the profound personal uncertainty I was already drowning in.

I was barely learning how to grieve one life when the world began grieving its own typical existence.

As schools shuttered and routines crumbled, I found myself adrift in a cold, vast sea of isolation. Purpose, once so firmly rooted in action and interaction, became as elusive as the sensation in my fingertips. The world had suddenly, eerily aligned with my experience. Everyone now lived in a state of shared uncertainty, their lives circumscribed by invisible threats and unfamiliar limitations.

The roles that had always anchored my identity—teacher, mother, writer, and entrepreneur—felt increasingly distant, almost ghostly. Writing demanded a focus I often couldn't summon. Teaching became impossible when I couldn't stand for long. Even motherhood, my most essential identity, became tangled in a fresh layer of grief.

Each limitation whispered a chilling lie: you're fading, you are not enough.

I was learning what many professionals quietly discover in crisis.

When your identity is tethered to performance, absence feels like unforgivable failure.

The isolation of lockdown amplified every struggle, until each one echoed through the vast, empty spaces of my days. Each hour forced me to confront questions I had been desperately avoiding. Who was I if I could no longer show up in the world as I once did? What value could I offer when my own body refused to cooperate?

A Lifeline Back to Myself

Desperation clung to me until, one especially dark afternoon, I reached for the phone and called Ann Marie, my friend and the Director of the Women's Business Center of Utah.

"Do you need any volunteers?" I asked, trying to steady my voice despite the raw, silent plea beneath it. Please, give me a reason to emerge from this isolation. Let me feel useful again.

Ann Marie's response came without hesitation. "Yes!" That single word threw me a lifeline. It wasn't just about having somewhere to be—it was about reconnecting with a world that felt increasingly distant and alien.

What began as a tentative offer to help soon evolved into something more. Volunteering transformed into a contract role, and before long, I found myself working part-time as a business advisor and instructor. Each step rekindled a vital spark. My body had limits, yes, but my mind and heart still held vast, untapped reservoirs of wisdom.

To an outsider, this new role might've looked like a total pivot. But the truth was far more nuanced. The very Core of who I was—my passion for growth, my enduring love of learning, and my innate drive to empower—remained intact. It had simply found a new, more adaptable container.

My husband and I had long juggled entrepreneurial projects—"Light-switch businesses" we could activate or pause as needed. They were more than mere survival strategies; they were agile expressions of our Core Values: freedom, creativity, and impact. Those ingrained lessons became a quiet, powerful preparation for the reinvention I hadn't seen coming.

So when Ann Marie offered me the role, I stepped in without hesitation. It wasn't just a job; it was a bridge—a lifeline back to engagement, a vital return to myself. It proved that I still had immense value to give, even in a life that looked nothing like the one I had meticulously planned.

I breathed a deep sigh of relief. I thought I had found purpose again.

But relief is not the same as freedom.

Beyond Usefulness

Inevitably, I caught myself doing what I had always done: tracking hours, checking boxes, striving relentlessly to prove I was pulling my weight. I had changed what I was doing but not why I thought I mattered.

Many leaders truly understand the trap of performance-based worth only when their ability to perform is challenged. I had adapted, yes, but had I truly changed?

If my value was perpetually tethered to usefulness, was that truly freedom?

And what about the women I worked with? Were they, too, measuring their worth by productivity? Quietly believing that only ceaseless doing could justify their place in the world?

That's when it hit me, with the force of a revelation: this wasn't just my battle. This was the silent standard we were all living under.

We weren't just
trying to shine—
we were trying
to earn the
right to shine.

We weren't just adapting—we were exhausting ourselves proving we still had value.

And the real loss wasn't just in what we could no longer do.

It was in forgetting that we were already enough.

But what if worth didn't depend on how brilliantly or how often we achieved something?

What if worth was—simply—steady as starLight, regardless of what we could or couldn't do?

Being Enough

Trusting that your worth is steady even when your output disappears.

Choosing presence over proving.

Remembering you are enough because of who you are, not what you do.

Chapter 5

Questions

When Metrics Fail, Meaning Calls.

From Doing to Being

Having walked through the deepest valleys of personal collapse and grief, I began to see my struggle was not unique. It was a microcosm of a larger societal challenge. My journey from doing to being led me to a crucial question, one that now reverberates across every profession and purpose-driven life.

Professionals are relentlessly trained to measure. Measure growth. Measure impact. Measure worth.

But what if the very systems we've built to define success are, in their silent precision, erasing something far more valuable?

Working with women entrepreneurs at the Business Center revealed stark, unsettling truths about how we measure value. The business formula seemed deceptively simple: worth equals problem-solving ability, measurable results, and tangible impact. Track the numbers. Monitor metrics. Count sales, followers, and engagement. Graph everything that moves.

But in those rooms, filled with both ambition and a quiet anxiety, I began to hear an echo—an unspoken pressure that mirrored the very one I had lived through in the MRI machine. As I guided these women through their entrepreneurial challenges, watching them wrestle with both the practical and existential questions about their worth, I began to see something alarming: the same invisible weight I felt in my diagnosis was relentlessly following them too. The language was different—revenue goals instead of physical milestones—but the deep ache underneath was identical.

That's when the realization hit me, with the force of a cold wave: I had bought into the same lie.

The Metric Fixation

I began seeing the deep, inherent flaws in this reductive equation. Our society's obsession with measurement has insidiously infiltrated every aspect of human experience, fundamentally transforming how we view worth and achievement. From our first day of school, we're initiated into what author Jerry Z. Muller calls the metric fixation—a relentless system of quantification that brutally reduces the richness of human potential to a mere series of numbers. Intelligence becomes a standardized test score. Creativity shrinks to fit a rubric. Professional value distills into performance indicators that flash across screens like frantic stock market tickers.

This quantification epidemic spreads far beyond education. In healthcare, doctors rush through appointments, checking boxes instead of truly seeing patients, their eyes fixed on screens rather than the complex humans before them.

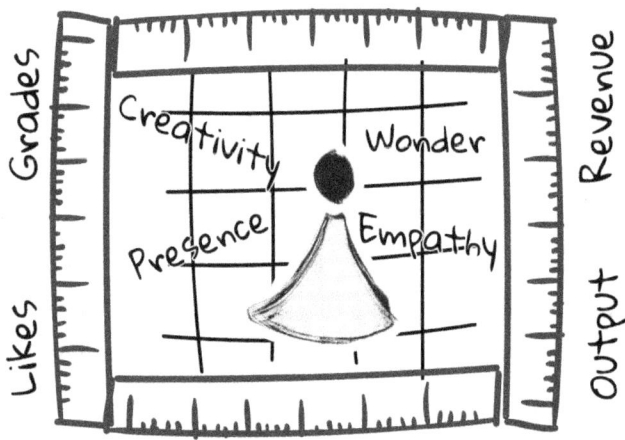

The Metric Fixation:

When systems meant to measure progress begin to define it, we lose what we're meant to protect.

Universities evaluate professors not by their ability to ignite intellectual passion, but by how often they're cited in academic journals. Businesses sacrifice long-term wisdom for the immediate, fleeting gratification of quarterly targets. Each number, ranking, and score doesn't just measure our world—it aggressively reshapes it, forcing us to prioritize what can be counted over what truly counts. And for leaders and changemakers, this systemic shift can quietly, fundamentally corrode the very things that make their work meaningful: intuition, empathy, and courage.

As Douglas Rushkoff observes, in our present shock culture—where everything is happening and being tracked now—we begin to lose our sense of narrative, depth, and meaning itself. We become so consumed by metrics that we forget that they were originally designed to serve the human spirit.

I had internalized this system long before I ever thought to question it. As a teacher, I obsessed over test scores and benchmarks, utterly convinced they truly captured learning and growth. As an entrepreneur, I relentlessly chased revenue targets and productivity goals, certain they could quantify my every success. Even in my personal life, I tracked walking times, logged fitness goals, and filled my planner with color-coded rows of checkboxes that offered the illusion of progress.

These numbers gave me a powerful sense of control, a tangible way to mark time and direction in a chaotic world.

But what began as comforting milestones soon hardened into rigid expectations. Performance reviews determined which dreams would be supported and which would be coldly shelved. Credit scores dictated access to everything from apartments to opportunity. Every achievement invited a new, more demanding metric, each one more relentless than the last. The goalposts didn't just move—they vanished into the distant horizon, no matter how fast or hard I ran.

Then came the MRI, with its own cruel mathematics. Seventeen lesions on my brain. Four on my spine. Each one was a cold, hard data point threatening to brutally define my future in clinical, dispassionate terms. Numbers that once offered clarity and validation now felt like merciless prophecies, detached, unfeeling.

I had spent years believing that the right numbers could protect me—from failure, from obscurity, from fear. But in that unforgiving machine, I saw the lie laid bare.

Metrics, once comforting, became suffocating.

These very tools I had trusted to measure progress suddenly turned on me, raising haunting, undeniable questions. What happens when the numbers fail us, when the very system we've used to measure our worth proves utterly inadequate?

That day in the MRI machine marked a searing, undeniable turning point.

For the first time, the numbers didn't reassure me—they erased me.

My teaching evaluations, my pace times, my business analytics—all the data points I had desperately clung to—now looked like false anchors in an unpredictable, raging sea. They couldn't measure the fear coursing through my veins, the crippling uncertainty clouding my thoughts, or the raw, exposed vulnerability that followed me home. No spreadsheet could account for the sleepless nights or the flickering, stubborn waves of hope that somehow survived each brutal setback.

Worse still, none of them could quantify resilience.

They couldn't measure the parts of me that remained whole, even when my body rebelled. They couldn't capture the stubborn, unyielding Light inside me—the part that profoundly refused to be reduced to an equation.

Beyond Numbers

As positive psychologist Barbara Fredrickson reminds us, it is hope, joy, and love—not productivity—that expand our capacity to cope and grow. Her broaden-and-build theory suggests that unmeasurable emotions are what enable us to adapt, endure, and thrive in the face of adversity. These were the forces rebuilding me, but no performance review could observe them.

But still, I tried. I diligently filled out spreadsheets. Tracked analytics. Counted hours worked and tasks completed. My planner was full again. My time meticulously accounted for. I was moving—busy, productive, undeniably measurable.

Yet something in me felt brittle, on the verge of splintering. The structure I had rebuilt was clean, efficient, and ultimately hollow. I had changed the numbers. But I hadn't changed the fundamental story I was telling myself about my worth. And in the profound stillness between metrics, I felt it—the quiet ache that whispered, This isn't it. This isn't enough.

And if the numbers no longer mattered, I had to ask the most terrifying, liberating question of all: what did? Because I had never just been what I could accomplish.

That question didn't strip me down; it set me free.

I was no longer desperately building my identity on output. I was remembering, slowly, beautifully, who I had always been underneath it all.

That's when I knew, with an unshakeable certainty: the metrics weren't just insufficient; they were irrelevant.

Excavation and StarLight

But knowing worth is intrinsic doesn't mean I could automatically live from that place. For years, I had blurred the line between who I was and what I did. Actions, roles, achievements—they felt like proof of my value. Without them, I felt hollow. Untangling that illusion was agonizing.

It wasn't enough to simply affirm, "You are valuable anyway." I had to prove it to myself in a different way—not by what I could do, but by what was already there. That's when I began the work of excavation: separating essence from evidence.

I sat down with a blank page, determined to name what was at my Core. Pen in hand, I was sure it would come easily. After all, I had spent a lifetime measuring myself. But when I tried to write "Compassion" or "Creativity," my mind immediately argued back, That's what you do in teaching. That's what shows up in business. That's tied to a role, not your essence.

Frustrated, I wrote instead: Teacher. Writer. Entrepreneur. Titles. Accomplishments. Outputs. I filled the page with them, only to feel a fresh ache. These were not essence. They were evidence.

In anger, I began crossing them out, line after line, until only white space stared back at me.

That empty page told the truth more clearly than anything I had written: my worth couldn't be captured by roles or scores or metrics. What remained was harder to name, but it was there—stubborn, unyielding, steady as starlight.

I started calling this part of me "my starlight." Like the fusion at a star's Core, these values burned with a steady, unearned brilliance.

My essence wasn't something I had to hustle to maintain. It simply was.

And if I could trust it, it could guide me—not as a metric to chase, but as a constellation to navigate by.

The realization didn't come as a thunderclap. It arrived like starLight—quiet, persistent, undeniable. But once it appeared, I couldn't unsee it: my value was never contingent on output. It was never earned through effort or proven through numbers. It was intrinsic. Immutable.

It had always been there—steady as a star—even when I had forgotten.

Just as a star's brightness is not determined by how we perceive it from Earth, our worth isn't dependent on external recognition or visible results. A star's Light begins in fusion, a powerful process at its Core. In the same way, our inner Light—our creativity, resourcefulness, courage, and faith—is the fusion of our Core Values. It burns regardless of our surroundings. It burns because of who we are.

This was the true beginning of my unraveling from performance to presence. And as the systems I once trusted fell silent, a quiet, profound remaking began. The summer became a surreal blend of monotony and slow, deliberate transformation, each day familiar yet utterly strange, steady yet quietly reshaping me from the inside out. That slow shift left me with a new essential question. How do you honor that kind of worth—the kind that lives beyond numbers—when all the systems you've trusted fall silent?

The answer was not a better benchmark or a cleaner spreadsheet. The answer was a map, stitched not from certainty, but from starLight. This was the birth of the Constellation Map, and I knew the first step had to be the hardest, to begin the Excavation again and Name the Unmeasurable.

At first, the Map was simply that—a pattern of Lights. It showed where I'd been but not how to move forward. I could trace my strengths but not yet feel their gravity. The pieces existed, but they hadn't begun to sing together.

It wasn't until the metaphor arrived—until Light became a new language—that the Map came alive. It showed me my truth but still didn't tell me the math of my worth.

Being Enough

Releasing the lie that numbers define your worth.

Naming the essence beneath roles, outputs, and accolades.

Trusting your steady inner light—your starlight—as the truest measure of value.

Remember

Part II

In The Pieces,
You Find What Was Never Lost.

Chapter 6

Notice

Truth Hides in Plain Sight

The Wrong Equation

The scene appeared ordinary: scattered pencils, a half-empty juice glass, and the soft glow of her laptop screen casting shadows on my daughter's furrowed brow.

At first glance, it seemed like just another quiet night at home, a typical moment in the rhythm of our daily lives. But something about her frustration pierced me.

There was something familiar in her sigh, in the way she gripped the pencil, erased, rewrote, doubted.

The air seemed to thicken around her sigh—frustrated, weary—which held more than confusion. It held the weight of her self-doubt.

The struggle wasn't just with numbers—it was with her sense of worth. And for a flicker of a moment, I wasn't looking at her anymore. I was looking at a younger me.

How early do we learn to confuse performance with value? How early do we start shrinking to fit the boxes numbers build for us?

And that moment, simple and fleeting, changed everything for me. I realized that this wasn't just about math. It was about how we measure ourselves and how we allow those measurements to define us.

"Mom," she sighed, "I don't get absolute value. Why does negative five equal positive five? It doesn't make sense."

I leaned over her shoulder and looked at the problem on her screen: $|-5| = 5$.

At first, it seemed like just another math problem, one I'd solved countless times without a second thought. But as I stared at the equation, something shifted, a deeper understanding I hadn't considered in years.

Why would -5 equal 5? Why would a negative be treated like a positive?

Something in her voice, in that sigh, pulled me back to a hospital bed, to a monitor's steady beep, and to the aching question of who I was without the numbers.

Absolute value: the measure of a number's distance from zero, regardless of whether it's positive or negative. It was simple. But in that moment, it felt significant.

I leaned in, ready to explain it to her.

"The absolute value of -5 equals 5 because both numbers are five units away from zero," I said, drawing a number line on her notebook. "It's not about the sign; it's about the distance." My finger traced the line as I continued, "Think of zero as your starting point. Whether you walk five steps to the right or five steps to the left, you've traveled the same distance."

A New Metaphor of Worth

As I spoke the words aloud, something caught in my throat. It wasn't just about teaching math anymore—it was about finally finding language for a truth I hadn't known how to articulate. Could this be it? Could this little equation, this forgotten middle school lesson, hold the metaphor I'd been missing? That number line had more to say than I realized.

What if human worth worked the same way? What if all this time, I hadn't lost value, but I'd just moved in a different direction? What if our value wasn't determined by whether life pushed us into what felt like positive or negative territory? What if, like absolute value, our fundamental worth remained constant—not measured by direction, but by depth, by magnitude, by the strength it took to move at all?

The positive five was the high-achiever, spinning twelve plates; the negative five was the MS patient lying still in the MRI. And the Absolute Value was telling me the essential, inherent worth required to exist in either state was exactly the same.

The realization hit me with a physical ache. I felt the hum of the MRI again—the sterile chill, the steady mechanical thrum—and for the first time, I didn't hear failure. I heard proof. Proof that even here, motionless and undone, I was still equal in value to the woman who once outran exhaustion for a living.

The metaphor was deceptively simple, yet it cracked open everything I thought I knew about worth.

In the early 1980s, linguist George Lakoff and philosopher Mark Johnson set out to study something most of us never stop to notice: the everyday metaphors we use without thinking. Their work shows that metaphors are not just colorful turns of phrase. They are the very frameworks by which we understand and experience life.

Without even realizing it, we live inside metaphors. They guide how we think, how we act, and even how we judge ourselves. Some metaphors give life. "Life is a journey" can help us view setbacks as detours rather than dead ends. Others, like "Numbers don't lie," can quietly imprison us, reducing the richness of our humanity to a spreadsheet. The insight is that when we change our metaphors, we change the world we live in.

That's why this little math problem with my daughter struck me so deeply. It wasn't just about solving for x. It was about solving for me. In absolute value, I discovered a new metaphor, one that allowed me to reinterpret my life. No longer trapped inside the story that negative meant failure, I could finally see that my value or worth was steady, no matter the direction life took.

The beauty of this work is that it invites all of us to notice the metaphors we've inherited and to ask whether they still serve us. If "Life is a battle," no wonder we feel exhausted. If "Time is money," no wonder we feel perpetually in debt. But what if we chose new metaphors? What if "Life is a garden," or "Time is a gift"? What if worth is absolute value—constant, intrinsic, unshaken by the highs and lows?

When we shift the metaphor, we shift the meaning. And when we shift the meaning, we open up new ways of living.

Dr. Lisa Feldman Barrett's groundbreaking research powerfully supports this idea. Her studies reveal that our brains process experiences as either moving us toward or away from desired states, much like positive and negative numbers on a line. These directional shifts influence our emotions and choices, yes, but they do not define our essence. Our true value, she argues, lies not in the direction we're heading, but in how we navigate those shifts with resilience and meaning.

Just as absolute value measures magnitude without regard to direction, our Core human worth exists independently of life's ups and downs. Whether we're moving toward success or away from failure, whether we're soaring high or sinking low, our intrinsic value remains unchanged.

Rewriting the Measure

It's not about the direction we're headed, but the strength, resilience, and determination we carry with us through every step. In that moment, I realized our worth is not defined by the outcomes but by how we face whatever life throws our way. That thought didn't just land, it echoed, deep within me—something I had been slowly coming to understand since my diagnosis.

But now, for the first time, I had a metaphor that could support it. I had a question I could resonate with, not just an answer to recite.

How often do we let numbers dictate our sense of self? The scale tells us we're too much or not enough, reducing our bodies to a single, fluctuating size. The bank account whispers that we're falling short, equating our worth to the balance of our finances. The medical chart becomes a cold scorecard, calculating our limitations and defining us by what we can't do. Each number, each measurement, holds power over how we see ourselves, like invisible chains binding us to a narrow, incomplete version of who we are.

But in that moment, I began to question everything. What if we're more than the numbers that attempt to define us?

What if our value is something deeper—something that can't be reduced to a number?

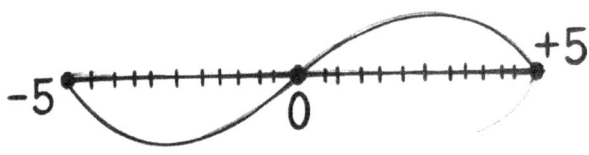

It's easy to let these numbers weigh us down, turning life's setbacks into judgments about our worth. We get caught in the belief that our value is tied to what we can quantify, what we can see.

But absolute value offers a different perspective. Just as −5 and 5 are equally distant from zero, we are equally valuable, no matter the positives and negatives of life.

Whether life feels like a triumph or a disaster, whether we're soaring high or sinking low, our worth remains constant. Like absolute value, it's not defined by where we are or how we feel in the moment but by the depth of our resilience, the strength within us that no number can capture.

In the end, our true worth lies in the quiet courage to keep going, the enduring capacity to rise after every fall, and the unwavering strength that utterly refuses to be measured by anyone's scale.

Just as a star's worth isn't determined by how brightly we perceive it,.

Our value isn't defined by recognition or setbacks.

Like a star's Light, it emanates from within.

This doesn't mean we never change. Stars evolve. So do we. But the fusion at our Core—the integration of our strengths, values, and lived Light—is what sustains us. My creativity, my resourcefulness, my love of teaching—these were my Light. And they remained, even when my performance fell away.

This understanding arrived not in a classroom or from a textbook but through a child's sigh, a pencil-marked number line, and the sacred ordinariness of showing up when things are hard. That evening had sparked a crucial understanding, but ideas don't change us until they collide with real life. And real life was messy, full of old stories and deeply buried beliefs. I didn't know it then, but the next part of my journey would unearth those stories—report cards, performance reviews, old comparisons—and reveal just how far this new understanding had to reach.

Witness: The Moment of Naming

Not long after, another ordinary moment brought the lesson home. In the severe brightness of my bathroom, I felt reduced again to a label on a bottle—MS patient. Fragile. Dependent. The mirror was merciless, the Light too honest. My reflection looked like a stranger—someone diminished, held together by routine and sheer will.

Then Wally stepped in. He didn't flinch from what he saw. He wrapped his arms around my waist, grounding me in a tenderness that didn't demand anything. His brown eyes—mischievous, steady—met mine in the mirror.

"You've always been one of the most determined people I know," he said quietly. "I still see that in you."

For a moment, I couldn't breathe. The word determined hit like both a memory and a mercy. It was the echo of the woman I used to be, and the truth of the one who remained. I felt something inside me rearrange, a tectonic shift beneath the surface. The sterile labels—MS patient, fragile, dependent—began to crack, their authority dissolving in the simple warmth of his conviction.

He wasn't naming what I could do. He was naming what had never left. Determination. Resilience. Steadiness.

That was the moment my excavation finally broke open. I wasn't inventing my Core—I was remembering it, confirmed by someone who had seen it in me all along.

That night, I finally wrote my Core qualities down: Courage. Creativity. Resilience. Faith. Determination.

Not roles. Not outputs. Not titles. My starLight.

The relief of naming them washed over me, but almost instantly, a new question arose. Now that I know who I am, how do I live it?

The evening with my daughter had ignited an inspired, profound understanding, and the Absolute Value metaphor gave me the language for comprehending my new worth, but it was still just a theory. I still had to undertake another part of my journey—the deepest part—to eradicate those old stories, the report cards, performance reviews, and buried comparisons that still defined my daily decisions. This new understanding had to reach the very roots of who I thought I was.

Being Enough

Choosing compassion over perfectionism when setbacks arise.

Speaking to yourself with the same kindness you offer others.

Living from your starlight instead of chasing proof through performance.

Chapter 7

Remember

*Your Worth Has Always Been More
than Numbers or Titles*

Unpredictable Ground

Some mornings, my legs cooperate. Other mornings, they forget. My body has become an unpredictable companion, one that can turn on me without warning.

I never know what will happen next. Will I walk across the room without help, or will my knees buckle halfway there? Will my hands hold steady or tremble when I reach for the toothpaste? Every day feels like opening a door to weather I can't predict.

That morning that Wally found me in the bathroom and reminded me of internal, eternal essence was the moment something in me broke open—not in collapse, but in revelation. I realized I wasn't inventing my Core; I was remembering it. And I wasn't remembering alone. Someone else had seen it too.

For years, I had trusted numbers to tell me who I was—grades, goals, reviews, outcomes. They were my compass, my scoreboard, my worth. Until one day, they stopped making sense.

I can still see myself at twelve, standing in the living room clutching a report card heavy with B's. My siblings' A's shone like spotLights beside me. The room felt too quiet. Each letter on that page seemed to shrink me smaller. Even then, I understood: I was being measured but not fully seen. I wasn't the smartest, but I was kind. And no report card could assess that.

That's where the seed was planted. Maybe you'll never be enough until you can prove it. So I tried to prove it everywhere I went—through leadership titles, glowing reviews, perfect grades. Even later, as a teacher, I confirmed my belonging in student test scores and parent praise. It didn't look like striving; it looked like purpose. But beneath it all, the same quiet ache kept whispering: earn it, earn it, earn it.

Then came my diagnosis. A new kind of report card—lesion counts, mobility scores, functionality ratings. Numbers that tracked not what I was gaining, but what I was losing.

The same systems that once made me feel accomplished now charted my decline. And I realized, maybe for the first time, that I had built my sense of worth on something that could crumble.

It felt like standing in a hallway between two selves—one I no longer was, and one I didn't yet understand. And in that in-between space, something ancient stirred.

That's when the Absolute Value metaphor came to life again. What had once been a simple math lesson for my daughter began to mirror my own truth.

Since absolute value measures distance from zero—how far something is from the center—then whether it's positive or negative, its relationship to the center remains the same. Zero isn't emptiness—it's origin. The still point. The unchanging Core.

My worth had never fluctuated. It had always been there—steady, rooted, constant—no matter which direction life pulled me.

The Practice Comes Through Loss

I wish I could tell you that realization was enough, that once I understood it, I lived from it easily. But truth rarely works that way. It has to make its way from the mind into the body, and sometimes, the journey hurts.

Even with all my clarity, something inside me still hesitated. My soul had caught up to the truth, but my nervous system hadn't. So life, as it often does, gave me a test.

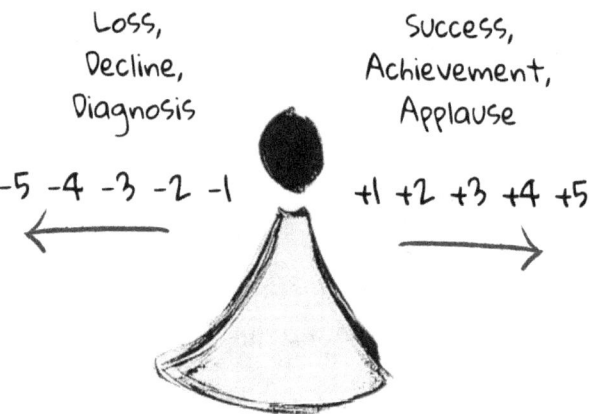

Absolute Value

Loss, Decline, Diagnosis

Success, Achievement, Applause

-5 -4 -3 -2 -1   +1 +2 +3 +4 +5

It's not the positives or negatives that matter—only your relationship to your Core.

One night, raw from exhaustion, I stepped outside and looked up at the stars. I wanted something I couldn't name—proof, maybe, or peace. But as I stood there, I felt a quiet recognition rise. The stars weren't performing. They weren't trying to earn their Light. They were simply being.

Their brilliance wasn't achieved. It was remembered.

Days later, a professional setback came—a cancelled event I'd poured my whole heart into. Instantly, my old programming roared to life. You should have planned better. You should have tried harder. You're failing. Everyone will see it.

For years, that voice had run my life. But this time, I caught it mid-sentence. I could hear the child behind it, still clutching her report card, still waiting to be told she was enough. So I asked myself, What would my starlight choose here? The answer wasn't performance. It was compassion.

Compassion for myself. For my team. Even for the disappointment itself.

Compassion is how my Core moves through the world—its faith steadying my tone, resilience softening into presence, creativity searching for Light when the room feels dark.

So, I chose differently. I called my team, not to apologize, but to thank them for showing up so fully. I rested instead of punishing myself with another twelve-hour day. And I whispered words I had rarely dared to say out loud. My worth hasn't changed.

No one else noticed. But inside, it felt seismic. For the first time,

I didn't just remember my worth, I lived like I believed it.

StarLight Remembered

Since then, I've seen the same pattern in the women I mentor. They measure their success in outcomes—clients, followers, income—but I watch them shine most brightly in the spaces no one measures: in their integrity, in their resilience, in their quiet courage to keep showing up.

One woman comes to mind. Her revenue was modest, but her Light was unstoppable. She built her dream one faithful brick at a time, fueled not by applause, but by conviction. Her value wasn't in the numbers. It was in the way she moved through the world.

That was success. That was enough.

Watching her reminded me of my own return to center. We were both practicing the same quiet act of remembering.

What I was reclaiming wasn't new. It had always been there, steady beneath the noise. Like a star, my worth didn't depend on who noticed or how brightly it burned from afar. It radiated from within—the fusion of creativity, faith, and resilience at my Core.

Now, when setbacks come—and they still do—I remind myself of this.

I am not my output. I am not my title. I am not my numbers.

I am the Light that existed before the measuring began. And in that remembering, I have come home.

Being Enough

Meeting yourself with compassion instead of criticism.

Letting kindness become your inner language.

Trusting that your light does not dim when you release perfection.

Chapter 8

Trust

The Stars Don't Change When the Sky Gets Dark.

What the Stars Remind Us

T here are moments when logic fails, when numbers fall short, and only the stars can help us remember who we are. This chapter is for anyone who has ever wondered if their Light still matters when roles shift, metrics fall away, and identity feels uncertain. It's not about finding your worth again; it's about trusting it was never gone.

One restless night, burdened by these questions, I wandered into the backyard. I lay on the damp grass, pressing my back against it, watching the stars slowly emerge in the darkening sky. Each one was unique—a red giant, a blue dwarf, a white neutron star—each burning with its distinct brilliance, yet all played essential roles in the vast, intricate patterns unfolding above. As I gazed up, I realized that despite their differences, every star contributed to something larger than itself, forming a cosmic design that couldn't exist without each individual Light. Some burned quietly. Some flared bright. But none apologized for the Light they offered, and none needed permission to belong to the sky.

I remembered teaching my kids about stars years before. "Each star's color tells us what it's made of," I'd explained, watching their eyes Light up with curiosity. "It's what they're made of that determines how they shine." They had been fascinated by the idea that we could learn so much about stars from millions of Light-years away, their brilliance reflecting their deepest qualities.

As I lay there, a lump formed in my throat, tightening with a question I couldn't ignore. When was the last time I'd felt certain about my own worth—and not just when things were going well? The answer was a chilling silence.

In those days, I didn't feel like someone brimming with Light or purpose. I felt more like a dying star, my brilliance dimming with each new limitation life threw my way. And the more I tried to grasp that dwindling sense of worth, the further it seemed to slip from my fingers, leaving me to wonder if it was ever truly mine to begin with.

The realization didn't creep in. It cracked through me like thunder, sudden and impossible to ignore. The question wasn't, "Where had my Light gone?"—it was, "When did I stop trusting that it was still there?" One moment I was lying still, the next I was upright, breath caught in my throat. My vision swam, but my thoughts had never been clearer. Had I been measuring my value through someone else's lens? A lens shaped by a world that valued output more than essence? By systems, expectations, and the demand for survival?

And yet, beneath the disorientation, a quiet spark lit inside me. What if there was another way to see value?

Not as something earned or measured but something I'd carried all along?

Stars aren't valued by their surface radiance. Astronomers look to the Core—the fusion, the essence, the unique makeup. Our worth works the same way. The shimmering brilliance we see is often just the surface, the illusion of distance. True stellar value lies in the Core, in the distinct composition, in the way a star interacts with the vastness of the universe.

Just like hydrogen and helium fuse to make light, your Core Values—the very essence of who you are—are what make you shine.

Just as a star's hydrogen and helium cause it to shine, the Core of who you are—the fusion of your values, faith, and resilience—causes you to shine. The Light isn't manufactured; it's generated from within.

The Role Villain Returns

The invitation arrived like a dare; a local entrepreneurship summit wanted me back on stage. My name was slotted in the program under three old titles: Speaker. Author. Leader. The email landed and, with it, the old anxiety—swift, practiced, and precise.

My mind started the familiar chant. You've been out too long. You'll stumble. You'll forget. You don't deserve to burn here. I could feel the old programming, and it wasn't subtle. It announced itself with the metallic taste of adrenaline and a spreadsheet of imagined judgments: attendance numbers, post-event surveys, social mentions. Performance disguising itself as safety.

I printed the brochure anyway and set it on the counter. For a while, I just stared at my name. The titles stared back.

Somewhere underneath the noise, a sentence surfaced, the witness that had cracked my excavation open months earlier. Wally's voice, steady as a heartbeat. "You've always been one of the most determined people I know. I still see that in you." He hadn't named a role. He'd named my Core.

What if the title isn't a verdict? What if it's just a vessel?
The Container

The realization arrived in a single, simple image: a title is a candle. My Core—creativity, faith, resilience—is the flame.

The candle gives the flame form and focus; it holds the wax that fuels the Light, helping it illuminate where it's needed. But the value isn't in the candle itself—it's in the fire.

If the candle melts, changes shape, or burns out, the flame can be transferred. It can Light another wick. It can kindle a new candle. The flame remains. The flame endures.

I looked back at the brochure. The speaker wasn't me. It was a candle. The author wasn't me. It was a candle. The leader wasn't me. It was a candle.

Suddenly, the old villain shrank. The Role had never been a judge or a jailer. It was only a vessel, a temporary form that allowed the same enduring flame to reach others.

The day of the summit, I arrived early. Backstage smelled like coffee and nerves. Techs adjusted the lights. Someone handed me a mic and a timer. The stage manager asked for my slides. I told her I didn't need them. She blinked, then smiled.

The old reflex reached for perfectionism. You always use slides. Hit the beats. Prove you still can. My chest tightened. I set a hand over my heart—not to still it, but to listen.

If the Role is a container, what do I light right now? Creativity: presence over polish. Faith: trust message over metrics. Resilience: let imperfection be a sign of life.

When they called my name, I stepped into the light—not to be measured, but to be of use. I didn't count heads. I found faces. I told the truth, not a highlight reel but a map drawn from the valleys. I spoke about what outlasts the quarterly report and about building cultures where people are more than output. I named the thing I had once been terrified to say out loud.

Your title is a tool, not a trophy. Don't protect the candle— protect the flame.

There was a stillness I know well, the kind that means the room had stopped grading and started receiving.

During Q&A, a founder with tears in her eyes asked, "But what am I without my company?" I didn't give her a strategy. I gave her back her essence. "You are the fire. Let the next container fit you, not fix you."

The Container

A role is only a container.
When it shifts or fades, your light
doesn't disappear—
it simply finds a new place to shine.

Afterward, I didn't check the survey link. I went to the lobby and sat with people. We swapped stories, the unglamorous, human kind. This is what roles are for, I thought. Not to make points but for pouring.

StarLight Remembered

As I saw this pattern emerge, the math started to make sense. Worth wasn't a single number, easily calculated or assigned. It was a constant relationship to our Core, expressed through the shifting ways we interact with the world. Like stars forming constellations, our individual Lights come together to create patterns far greater than ourselves, each contributing to a larger, more meaningful whole.

Tomorrow will still bring challenges. The medical metrics won't magically change. But I can face them differently now, trusting that my worth—like absolute value—remains constant, regardless of external measures. The stars hadn't changed. I had simply learned where to look and how to move.

Trust: The Final Act

Trust, I realized, is not passive belief. Trust is use. It's taking your flame into the world again, on purpose, without bargaining for safety or applause.

So I made one small, public commitment the next morning. Not a rebrand, not a launch. A yes, that would have terrified the old me for its lack of metrics. I agreed to mentor a cohort of first-time founders with no speaking fee, no social footprint attached, and no deliverable other than presence. Not to disappear into service but to express the Core in a role that fits my life now. Another container. Same flame.

I sent the email and closed my laptop. No rush of performance high. No crash either. Just that grounded, lucid feeling I used to call faith when I was younger, now mixed with the steady pulse of resilience.

Creativity hummed again, not like fireworks, but like a pilot light.

The titles I carry from here are just candles—each one burning for a time, shaped for a purpose. If one melts, another will be lit. And if none remain, the flame itself will still exist—steady, untouchable, enough.

Being Enough

Trusting that your core is the light and roles are only containers.

Letting titles serve as tools rather than trophies.

Moving into roles from presence and alignment, not performance.

Chapter 9

Name

*Language Gives Shape to What We
Already Know*

Back to the Begining

What if your deepest worth was never in what you
have accomplished but in who you've always
been?

In a world where so many professionals assess identity through roles, output, and achievement, this chapter is an invitation to come back to the Core—to name who you are, to remember, not reinvent.

"If God had given you a calling before you were born, what would it be?"

My friend Carol's question hung in the air between us—earnest, unexpected, and gently probing. We were sitting in my yard, sipping herbal tea as the afternoon Light filtered through the leaves. It was one of those rare moments of stillness in the midst of the upheaval my MS diagnosis had brought.

I set my teacup on my lap, considering. Who was I now that my body had betrayed me? What worth did I have when I could no longer be the teacher, wife, or mother I once was? Carol's question cut through to the heart of my searching.

"I...I don't know," I admitted.

The answer seemed to hover just beyond my reach, obscured by layers of roles and expectations I had worn for so long.

Carol smiled gently. "That's okay. Sit with it. You don't have to know right away."

And so I did. In the days and weeks that followed, I started peeling back those layers, examining each one in the Light of Carol's question. Slowly, tentatively, a single word began to take shape.

I remembered how a student had clung to my words that spring—how one had whispered, "You believed in me when no one else did."

Heartener. The word rose up within me with startling clarity one morning as I journaled. A combination of encourager, uplifter, and cheerleader. It wasn't a job title—it was a soul signature. It resonated in my bones. Heartening wasn't just something I did; it was how I brightened the world.

Heartener wasn't my Core itself—it was my shine, the way my Core elements of faith, courage, and creativity came together and spilled into the cosmos.

Just as a star's hydrogen and helium ignite the fusion that makes it blaze, the Core of who you are—your deepest values, your essence—fuels your Light. The brilliance others see is simply the visible echo of that internal fire.

My roles did and would change, but the shine would outlast it all.

Naming the Core

This act of naming, of finding the precise language for an intrinsic truth, is profoundly transformative. As developmental psychologists and self-concept theorists have shown, articulating and embracing our authentic self, distinct from the roles we play or the expectations placed upon us, is crucial for psychological well-being and a robust sense of identity. It's about aligning with what Carl Rogers termed the "real self" rather than a conditional "ideal self" based on external validation.

I thought back to my teaching days, how I had always been drawn to the students who struggled most. It wasn't just about imparting knowledge; it was about helping them believe in themselves. Even with my own children, my deepest joy came from nurturing their unique gifts, fanning the flames of their passions.

And now, even as I navigated the uncertainty of my diagnosis, I found myself naturally falling into the role of heartener. I gravitated toward those who were losing hope, offering a listening ear and gentle reminders of their unshakable worth.

The realization brought tears to my eyes. All this time, I thought my value lay in the specific roles I played. But my true worth—my soul's calling—had been there all along, woven through everything I did.

It wasn't about what I achieved; it was about who I was.

But was this enough? In a world that measured worth by accomplishments, by titles, by tangible output, how could simply being a heartener possibly hold the same weight as my previous professional achievements? It felt too soft, too intangible, to be my calling before I was born—especially when the world so often rewarded only what could be counted.

I wrestled with the doubt. Could something so inherent, so quietly expressed, truly be the foundation of my value?

Faith. Courage. Creativity. These aren't just admirable traits; they are examples of the universal character strengths identified by positive psychologists like Christopher Peterson and Martin Seligman in their comprehensive VIA Classification of Strengths and Virtues. Their research demonstrates that these inherent, positive qualities are not merely skills but fundamental aspects of our being that enable us to thrive and lead meaningful lives, regardless of external circumstances.

As I examined this Core truth about myself, I saw how these values had always guided me, like a compass pointing true north. My faith—not just in God, but in the inherent potential of every person—was the bedrock on which my identity as a heartener stood. It gave me the courage to keep showing up, even on my hardest days, and fueled my creativity in finding new ways to uplift others.

These were my Core elements, the essential building blocks of my being. Recognizing them felt like coming home to myself, a long-awaited reunion with parts of me I'd almost forgotten. It was as though I'd been piecing together a puzzle, and finally, the picture was beginning to make sense.

From Naming to Living

But then a new question arose—one that stopped me in my tracks. What do I do with this knowledge?

The answer didn't come easily. At first, I tried to keep these insights to myself, believing they were a deeply personal map meant only to guide my own steps. Yet, as I began navigating life with these values at the forefront, I started to notice a ripple effect. My decisions became more intentional. And the Light of those choices didn't just guide me. It began to illuminate paths for others.

The realization was both thrilling and daunting. If this understanding could guide me so profoundly, what could it do for someone else?

But sharing these ideas wasn't as simple as I'd hoped. How could I translate something so intensely private into a message that others could grasp? How could I give them a glimpse of what it felt like to see their values as stars forming a guiding constellation?

I wrestled with these questions, feeling the weight of both possibility and responsibility. Yet, as I reflected on my own journey, I realized that my doubts weren't obstacles—they were invitations to grow. If I could frame my story in a way that resonated with others, perhaps they, too, could see their values as building blocks for a life filled with meaning and purpose.

Because naming alone isn't enough. A name is only a whisper until it's lived.

And living from that truth—claiming it, embodying it, and aligning with it—is the beginning of freedom.

So, I decided to take a leap.

I began to share—tentatively at first—in conversations with friends, in workshops, in written words. This act of inviting others to re-author their own understanding of worth, echoing principles found in narrative therapeutic practices, proved deeply resonant. To my amazement, people didn't just listen—they connected. They saw themselves in my story. They began to map their own constellations, Lighting up with the same sense of recognition I had felt.

Each name became a star. Each story, a dot of Light. And together, these constellations revealed a deeper truth—not just about who we were but about how we belonged. In naming ourselves, we weren't just remembering our authentic, eternal selves were. We were finding our place in something larger.

That's when it became clear. The act of sharing wasn't about imposing my truth—it was about inviting others to discover theirs. Like stars, our values are brightest when they illuminate not just ourselves, but the world around us. By sharing this understanding, I wasn't just coming home to myself—I was creating a space where others could come home to themselves too.

The Trap of Numbers

For years, I let numbers dictate my worth—grades, performance reviews, productivity charts. Maybe you have too. But here's the truth:

Numbers can track output but never essence.

Data might rise and fall; your worth does not.

Your resilience, your creativity, your compassion, your faith—these cannot be tallied or ranked. They are immeasurable, and yet they are the truest indication of who you've always been.

So, I ask you:

Who are you, beyond the numbers? What are the qualities that make you uniquely you, even when the metrics fail? What would your life look like if you led from those Core elements, instead of chasing proof of worth?

These are your Core elements. Your unshakable truths. They are your worth in a world that often forgets how to measure the immeasurable.

The science is clear, and these aren't a wish list. They are the building blocks of who you already are. Now it's your turn. In the workbook, you'll use the VIA framework to name your Core Elements—mapping the constellation of strengths that has always been within you. Don't skip this step. The work of remembering becomes real when you see it written in your own hand.

When you find and live from this place, you are free—not because the numbers go away, but because they no longer define you.

In a world ruled by numbers, you become something far more powerful. Someone who knows their worth without needing it to be counted.

This understanding—this remembering—is just the beginning.

Being Enough

Naming your soul's calling—your shine—as deeper than achievement.

Trusting your core values as your true compass.

Living your values out loud so they ripple beyond you.

Reclaim

Part III

You Begin Again, Not by Doing More,
But by Being You.

Chapter 10

Wrestle

Even Truth Takes Strength to Hold.

When Revelation Meets Reality

It began on an ordinary Tuesday.

I was curled up on the couch, laptop balanced across my legs, drafting words for this very book. Outside, a weak winter sun pressed through the blinds. Inside, the heater hummed, and the cursor blinked—a steady pulse on a blank page that refused to be filled.

I had already written about Absolute Value—how worth remains constant, even when life unravels. I didn't need convincing anymore; the revelation had taken root.

I knew who I was. I had named it, claimed it, and grieved what had buried it.

But knowing your worth and living from it are not the same thing.

That afternoon, the silence thickened, the kind that amplifies every breath, every heartbeat. Because reclaiming worth doesn't end with remembrance. It begins there.

Worth, I realized, isn't something you guard in thought. It's something you risk in motion. It's how you write the email, set the boundary, rest without apology, or show up when you can't fix a thing.

And that practice—living aligned with what I already knew—was the wrestle.

Remembering your worth is revelation. Living it is resistance.

I had done the inner work, but embodiment demanded something braver. Embodiment asked me to carry what I knew into moments that didn't mirror it—to hold my ground in stillness, limitation, and uncertainty, and live the truth anyway.

Suddenly, being a divine child wasn't comfort; it was accountability. It meant my words, my choices, even my energy, had to reflect what I already believed. It wasn't a truth to rest in—it was a way to walk.

Some days, that alignment came easily. Other days, I found myself slipping back into old equations, trying to earn what was already mine.

The wrestle wasn't doubt anymore. It was discipline.

It was the friction of learning to speak fluently in a language my soul had always known.

Because every revelation asks to be embodied, and embodiment always feels like tension before it feels like truth.

The wrestle is the space where remembrance becomes real, where worth stops being an idea and becomes a way of being.

The Physics of Worth

In that season, a new image rose in me like a slow dawn.

My Core is the center of a star—pure, steady, unchanging.

But starLight doesn't appear instantly. It travels through distance, dust, and time before it can be seen.

What we witness in the night sky isn't the Light's beginning—it's the proof of its persistence.

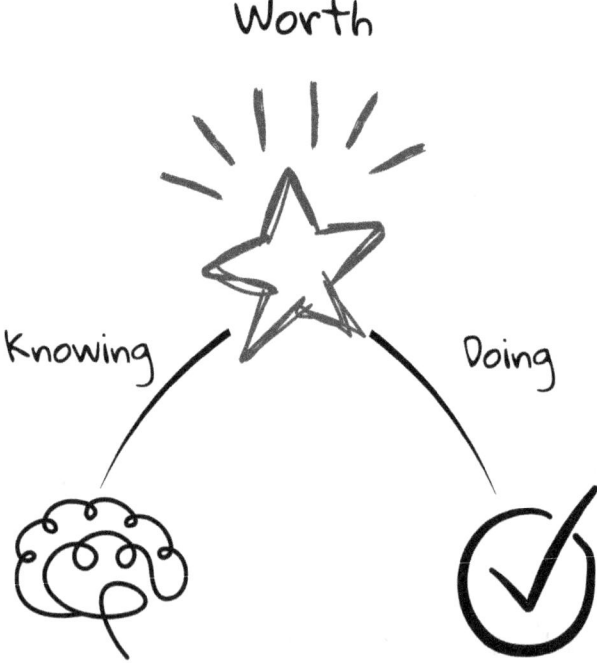

The gap between knowing and doing is where worth learns to grow.

Worth works the same way. The truth at your center never disappears. It simply takes time—and practice—for that Light to reach the surface of your life.

The moments you feel furthest from your worth aren't evidence of its loss.

They're evidence of its enduring motion.

So when the darkness feels endless—when your confidence flickers and your alignment wavers—remember: you're not losing your worth. You're learning how to live it.

The Moment After

Later that evening, I closed the laptop and sat in the dim Light of the living room. The heater had gone quiet. The sun had long disappeared.

For a moment, there was only stillness, a soft hum of something unseen but alive.

Then, almost on cue, the old voice returned. You should be working. You're falling behind. They'll think you've given up. The familiar ache of guilt rose like static, the reflex to validate myself by movement. I felt the tug, the urge to reopen the screen, to prove my worth one more time.

But I didn't move. I let the voice pass through me like wind against glass.

Outside, the moon was rising, slow and deliberate, slipping its silver through the blinds. It wasn't asking to be noticed; it simply was.

I watched the Light stretch across the floor and understood: this is what alignment feels like. Not shining harder. Not proving or performing. Just showing up—steady and true—the persistence of your Light, always arriving.

Being Enough

Holding the tension between what you know and what you can live.

Letting your light move through new forms without losing its source.

Trusting that resistance is not failure but part of creation.

Chapter 11

Subract

*Strip Away What Isn't You to Uncover
What Endures*

Surrender: When Life Cuts First

We've committed to the wrestle, to the hard, deliberate practice of living aligned with our worth. But how do we know what deserves our energy and what is just noise? How do we know what to keep and what to release?

This is where The Subtraction Effect becomes more than an idea—it becomes a way of living. It's the sacred discipline of letting go of what isn't true, so what's essential can finally rise. It's the practical work of clearing the deck so your Absolute Value can lead.

Subtraction shows up in two forms. Sometimes it's forced upon us by life. Other times, it's a choice we learn to make.

The first lesson in Subtract.is that even tiny acts of alignment can feel like enormous resistance. I knew that discipline began with a choice. My inbox, the place where the old equation of performance still lived, had become an altar of anxiety.

So, I subtracted it. I deleted the email app from my phone that morning. The screen went still, and the silence that followed felt almost rebellious—like dropping a twenty-pound weight I hadn't realized I was carrying. It wasn't dramatic, but it was decisive. And for the first time in a long while, the quiet felt like freedom.

The first kind of subtraction requires surrender—accepting the cuts life makes to your time, your energy, your ability.

My sister showed up one Saturday morning with paint cans, takeout, and that familiar look of quiet determination. She's an interior designer by trade, but that day she wasn't there as a professional. She had the weekend off and decided I could use some help.

"What do you want done?" she asked, already rolling up her sleeves.

Months earlier, I'd remodeled the house to add a handicap-accessible bathroom. The adjoining bedroom, though, was still unfinished—half-painted walls, holes in the ceiling, a pile of tools that stared at me every time I walked past. I had started the work myself, but somewhere between good intentions and exhaustion, my body drew a hard line.

When my sisters and I decide something needs doing, there's no stopping us. We're warrior women—strong, resourceful, a little stubborn. But this time, I couldn't be part of the charge. And that truth stung.

I watched my sister move easily around the room, occasionally balancing on a step stool, patching and sanding. Her body worked the way mine used to—fluid, certain, strong. Gratitude and grief mingled in my chest.

The old me would have pushed through the pain, worked until I collapsed, and refused to stop until every line was perfect. That version of me believed effort equaled worth. But she was gone.

So I sat on the edge of the bed, roller in hand, doing what I could. Paint a little. Rest. Paint again.

The room wasn't just changing color—it was shedding layers of who I used to be. Each stroke of paint felt like a small act of surrender, a release of everything I'd clung to: the need to prove, the impulse to overdo, the illusion that my value lived in motion.

I wasn't leading this project. I wasn't in control. I was being helped. And somehow, that was its own kind of healing.

The work was simple but holy. The cool drag of the roller across the wall felt cleaner than any mental battle I'd fought in months. And somewhere between the paint fumes and the music, something inside me softened.

Subtraction Effect

Subtraction doesn't make you less.
It makes you true.

My body, though limited, was alive. My heart, though grieving, was open.

Psychologist Barbara Fredrickson describes this as the broaden-and-build effect, explaining how moments of genuine positive emotion don't just feel good but widen our view and expand our capacity for resilience. Joy, even in small doses, broadens what's possible inside pain.

That day, the Light spilling across those blue walls did exactly that. It widened the room. It widened me.

By late afternoon, sunLight turned the fresh paint to Light. I stood in the doorway, exhausted and alive, watching my sister wash her brushes at the sink.

We had subtracted the unfinished, the forgotten, the parts left hanging. But beneath it all, we uncovered something deeper—a quieter, truer version of me that could let love in and let go.

When you accept the Subtraction life imposes, what remains after the cut isn't emptiness—it's resonance. That gentle hum is your Absolute Value, your truest self, vibrating free from the noise of proving.

Clarity: When You Choose the Cut

Not all Subtraction arrives gently. Sometimes clarity doesn't whisper—it scrapes. It comes wrapped in frustration and friction, demanding a conscious choice to take the knife yourself.

A few years ago, I worked with Trish, a brilliant woman building her own business. She wanted a brand that felt professional and inspiring, something that would stand out.

We began designing. She'd bring in mock-ups that looked polished, trendy, and perfectly impressive. But every time we finished one, she'd lean back, her shoulders clenched, and let out a weary sigh. "It's nice...but it's not me."

So we kept trying to perform our way to her truth. We added layers of visual noise—a custom typeface here, a flourish of color there, more texture, more move-ment—hoping one more addition would finally make the project click. But the harder we strained, the heavier the entire process felt.

It was effort without life.

The design was choking on its own aspiration.

By evening, Trish sat across from me, defeated. The frustration settled between us like palpable static. "I don't even know what I like anymore," she whispered quietly. "I just know none of this feels right."

I recognized the moment and the unmistakable sound of the Efficiency Trap collapsing under its own weight. I said the only thing left to say.

"Then let's erase everything."

She blinked, stunned. "Everything?"

"Everything," I confirmed. "We stop solving for the outside. Let's start with who you are—not what you think you should look like."

We began deleting one design after another until the screen was empty except for her name. Just plain, bold black text with a single, unadorned checkmark beside it.

For the first time that day, she didn't just sigh, she exhaled. Her shoulders dropped fully, and a genuine smile surfaced. "That's it," she breathed. "That's me."

The air felt Light, like the space itself had opened up. The pretending was gone. The noise had quieted. And in that stillness, what was true could finally surface.

That's the secret of this second kind of Subtraction: it doesn't strip you down—it brings you back.

What looks like emptiness is often freedom. And freedom, when it's real, feels like home.

The Invitation to Alignment

Mastery of The Subtraction Effect lives in a delicate, holy balance—the grace to accept the Subtraction of surrender when life limits you, and the courage to choose the Subtraction of clarity when your truth demands it.

Subtraction isn't surrendering to failure. It's choosing strength that no longer needs to prove itself.

I learned this one afternoon when I'd planned a simple dinner for Wally—nothing extravagant, just proof to myself that I could still manage normal. But halfway through chopping vegetables, my hands began to tremble. The knife slipped. My body whispered "no" long before I was willing to listen. The old me would have powered through, pushing past pain to preserve pride. Instead, I set the knife down, exhaled, and called him to bring takeout. It was such a small thing, but surrender never feels small when your worth used to exist in doing.

Every time you clear away what isn't true—a belief that shrinks you, a role that no longer fits, a rhythm of over-doing that leaves no room to breathe—you make space for what is essential to rise.

The goal isn't emptiness. The goal is alignment.

Stop spending your energy layering, performing, polishing, trying to earn what was never in question. True clarity doesn't come from adding more; it comes from releasing what's in the way.

Trust the quiet hum. Trust the clarity that comes through contrast. Trust the truth that remains when everything else has fallen away.

When you stop adding noise, you don't disappear—you finally emerge.

What's left after Subtraction isn't less. It's the whole, complete, enduring you.

Now that the space has been cleared, we can begin the sacred work of translation—giving form to the truth you've reclaimed.

Being Enough

Clearing what no longer fits so your truth can breathe.

Trusting friction as a teacher rather than a failure.

Choosing alignment over accumulation again and again.

Chapter 12

Shape

Begin to Intentionally Form that Light into Action.

The Gap

Worth is not a destination. It's a source.

We've been reminded of that source—the quiet, steady glow that defines who you are. But remembering is only the beginning. The final movement of this journey asks something deeper: to let what's true begin to take form.

Your worth is unchanging—a flawless diamond buried deep in the earth. But even a flawless diamond cannot change the landscape until someone chooses to cut and set it. Shape is the sacred act of translation. It's the way your inner Light learns to move through your life—the difference between potential for a masterpiece and actually picking up the brush.

Growth doesn't happen when you find the perfect expression. It happens when you begin to practice the truest one available to you right now.

For a long time, I believed that once I knew my worth, everything else would fall into place. That the world would somehow rearrange itself to match my new internal order. I thought the inner work—the grieving, the trusting, the remembering—was the finish line.

But when I tried to carry that luminous clarity into daily life, I ran straight into the gap— the wide, uneasy distance between what I knew to be true and how I could actually manifest it.

Every idea felt too heavy to lift. Every plan, too fragile to hold. I kept trying to rebuild what had been—the overflowing schedule, the quick momentum, the relentless pace— as if my old rhythm could somehow carry this new truth.

But all that motion wasn't meaning. It was just noise.

During a call with my mentor, I described a sprawling new project that sounded impressive on paper but would have devoured every ounce of energy I didn't have. She listened quietly, and when I finally paused for breath, she asked, "Are you trying to fit into the life you have now, or are you still trying to be the shape you used to be?"

The question sliced clean through my justifications.

Forcing vs Forming

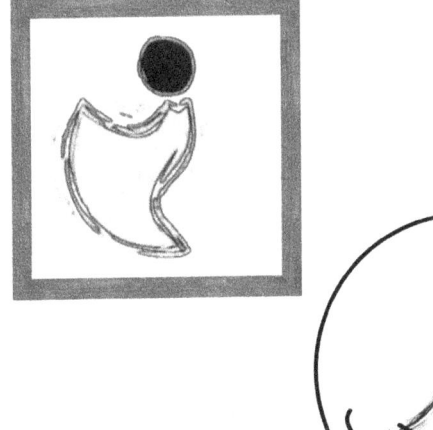

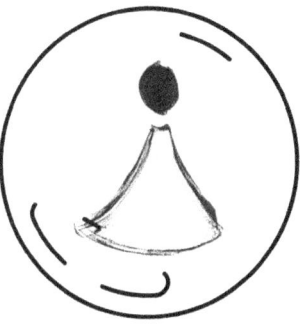

Stop forcing yourself into old shapes. Start forming the one that fits who you've become.

Because she was right. I wasn't shaping anything at all. I was straining—trying to cram my renewed, expanded self back into an old, rusted container. I was pretending alignment instead of practicing it.

That day, something in me loosened. I stopped trying to make the new fit the old. Shaping, I began to realize, isn't about rebuilding what was. It's about giving form to what is.

The Shape of Courage

True expression rarely begins with grandeur. It begins with alignment—small, honest choices that ripple outward in ways we can't predict. I've watched that quiet courage unfold in so many of the women I coach, but one story always brings it home.

Crystal has always felt music in her bones—alive, intuitive, uncontainable. As a teacher, she didn't just train young musicians, but she created spaces where children didn't just learn the violin—they belonged to it.

But that belonging didn't look like tradition.

Her approach—joyful, playful, rooted in movement—didn't match the polished, methodical systems that had shaped violin education for decades. Colleagues encouraged her to adjust, to refine, to make her methods more "professional." They wanted her to shape her teaching to match what had already been proven.

She began to doubt herself. Should she quiet the laughter and follow the old curriculum? Should she go back to the checklists that had been taught for decades? Both ways, her students would play the right notes—but with the old way, she knew something vital was missing. The sparkle. The pulse. The why.

One afternoon, she sat across from me, the weight of tradition heavy on her shoulders. "I don't know what to do. My mentors, the people I admire, encourage me to stay true to their methods."

I didn't offer a defense of her worth; we had already established that. I offered an invitation to shape.

"Well, what do you feel in your Core? What do you want your music school to be?"

The shift was immediate. "When I teach my way," she told me, her eyes bright, "they all Light up. And not just the kids—other teachers start trying it too. It's like their Light ignites mine."

That was her moment of shaping, when alignment stopped being an idea and became a choice of form.

She began to peel back everything that felt performative and returned to what was true. She brought play back into the room. She encouraged children to move, to listen, to laugh—to let joy become the teacher.

And when she did, something incredible happened.

Her eyes softened. "So it's not about being seen," she said quietly. "It's about helping others remember their own Light."

Exactly.

That's what it means to shape your Light. Not to perfect it, but to practice it. Not to force your impact but to live it so that your truth finds its distinct form in motion, and the world begins to glow a little brighter because you dared to be that shape.

The Discipline of Micro-Expressions

Shaping doesn't require a grand vision. It begins with micro-expressions—small, faithful experiments in living from your Core.

After that call with my mentor, I asked myself, "What is the smallest way I can live from what's true right now?"

My Core was clear: I exist to make people feel safe, seen, and strengthened.

But how could I live that when my energy was limited? I realized the answer wasn't to do more—it was to do less, on purpose.

My first act of shaping wasn't a launch, a post, or a speech. It was a boundary.

I blocked two quiet hours, four days a week, with no external obligations. At first, it felt reckless—like hiding when I should be producing. But I soon realized that say-ing "no" to what drained me was an act of service, not selfishness.

Old shape: making others feel safe by overextending myself. New practice: making others feel safe by modeling stability and rest.

For the first time, my remembered worth had found a working shape. It wasn't glamorous. It looked like a full afternoon of rest followed by one focused hour of writing. It looked like steadiness.

It looked like integrity in motion.

Practice, Not Perfection

Here's the truth: shaping is messy. It's supposed to be.

We often mistake the process for the product. We expect a sculpture on the first strike of the chisel. We forget that shaping anything—a life, a calling, a rhythm—requires iteration.

Think of the first time you picked up an instrument. The first sound wasn't harmony. It was noise. But you kept playing. You adjusted. You tried again.

The same is true here. Your first attempt at alignment will wobble. Your second might too. But practice—not perfection—is what turns truth into texture.

You're not being graded on the beauty of your outcome. You're being shaped by the honesty of your effort.

Every small act of congruence—every time your outer life catches up to your inner knowing—is the sacred work of becoming.

You do not
have to perfect
your purpose.
You only have
to practice it.

Shape is not performance—it's devotion. It's the ongoing, imperfect translation of your Light into the world.

Let it take time. Let it look unfinished. Let it sound off-key at first.

Because every act of shaping, no matter how small, is proof that your worth has found breath again.

And that is enough.

Being Enough

Letting what's true take shape through practice rather than perfection.

Choosing integrity over image and alignment over applause.

Translating your inner light into small, honest actions that serve.

Chapter 13

Harmonize

Blend Values, Find Personal Rhythm,
Unlock New Strength

Overlap

The morning sun streamed through my window, catching on the crystal wind chimes above the sill. Beams of Light refracted into vibrant streaks of color, scattering across the walls and ceiling like fragments of a broken rainbow. For a moment, the room felt alive with quiet magic, as if Light itself was trying to remind me that beauty could still find its way into fractured places.

I sat at the kitchen table, mesmerized by it, even as my body felt heavy, weighted by the relentless hum of an MS flare. It wasn't a sharp pain so much as a quiet siege, a constant, invisible current that made even breathing feel like work.

Earlier that week, I had dropped a glass. The day before, a full mug of tea. Small moments, but they landed like losses. Each one seemed to announce what was slipping through my grasp: independence, confidence, identity. The ache wasn't only in my hands. It pulsed through everything I could no longer hold.

My hand slid into my lap. I sank deeper into the chair, staring at the coffee mug in front of me. It looked harmless enough, but in that moment, it felt like a test I hadn't studied for. My only mission for the next ten minutes was to lift it without spilling. Even the smallest acts had become monumental challenges, each one a sharp-edged reminder of what I had lost.

Frustration rose hot in my chest, that familiar mix of shame and defiance. I saw myself as a list of failures: shaky hands, canceled plans, a shrinking version of someone I used to know. I was tired of measuring my life in spills.

And then something flickered.

The sunLight caught the wind chimes again. Color fractured and reassembled across the room. Tiny rainbows danced on the walls, shimmering with the faintest movement of air. Where the colors overlapped, new hues appeared—soft, fleeting, and impossibly beautiful.

For a moment, I forgot the ache. I just watched. And somewhere between the Light and the stillness, a small, quiet truth began to rise in me.

> Maybe the breaking wasn't the end of beauty. Maybe it was how the Light got in.

The word came like a whisper, small but insistent.

Maybe my values—courage, creativity, faith, empathy—weren't meant to stand alone. Maybe, like those scattered beams of Light, their real brilliance appeared only when they met and mingled. Maybe Value Fusion wasn't about choosing one trait to lead but letting many traits work together to create something new—possibilities that couldn't exist in isolation. Their strength, I realized, came through connection.

I reached for the mug again, this time with both hands. My fingers curled around the handle, unsteady but deliberate. I braced my elbows on the table and steadied myself. Slowly, carefully, I lifted the mug. Warmth spread through my palms—a small, quiet victory.

Courage alone hadn't carried me that morning. It had needed adaptability to meet me where I was. Together, they harmonized into a new kind of strength, one greater than the sum of its parts.

That small moment opened something wider. I thought of other times my values had fused to carry me through—when faith and creativity joined forces so I could stay connected with loved ones even when my body couldn't keep up, when empathy and determination intertwined, helping me support others while still standing up for myself.

Wholeness, I realized, is a rhythm, not a checklist.

When you stop treating your values as separate tools and begin blending them with intention, something powerful shifts. You move through challenges with grace instead of striving, with harmony instead of hierarchy. That fusion becomes your personal rhythm of resilience, creativity, and strength.

Your values are living threads. When woven together with care, they don't just hold you together. They hold the Light that leads others forward.

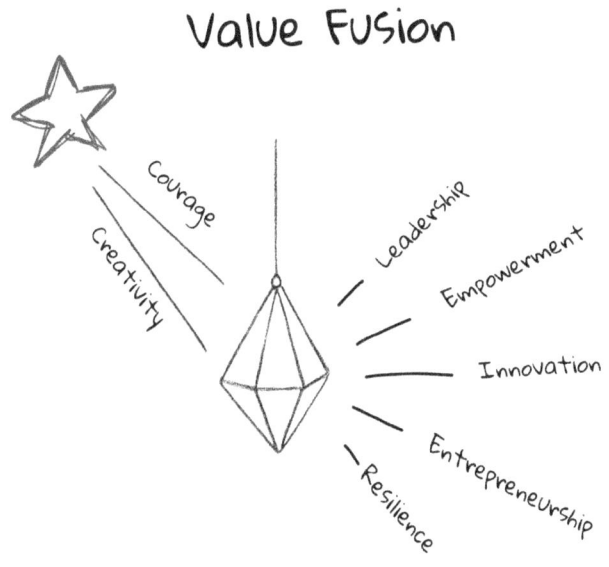

Value Fusion

Courage

Creativity

Leadership

Empowerment

Innovation

Entrepreneurship

Resilience

Where light overlaps, new colors are born.

The Constellation Effect

When you fuse your intrinsic values, you don't just achieve resilience; you create a stable pattern of Light—one that guides not only you but those who are searching in the dark.

I call this The Constellation Effect.

Your brilliance doesn't come from a single, isolated element. It comes from the fusion of your truths under pressure. Like the fiery Core of a star fusing hydrogen and helium, the process of Value Fusion creates something far more powerful than any single strength on its own. This is the difference between a solitary flicker and an undeniable, consistent guiding Light.

We see this same cosmic-level fusion in the people who have illuminated history.

Mahatma Gandhi's strength wasn't just truth; it was the blending of truth with humility, compassion, and political strategy. His humility didn't lessen his power; it amplified his message, allowing his integrated values to move nations.

Dr. Martin Luther King Jr.'s brilliance wasn't just conviction; it shone through the harmonizing of fierce courage with grounding empathy and unflinching justice. His courage was rooted in love, not ego, allowing him to bear the weight of injustice while still believing in the humanity of those who opposed him.

This kind of fusion is the key to deep, enduring impact. Studies on value integration confirm that people who consciously blend their strengths report greater adaptability and satisfaction, especially in times of adversity. When we view challenges as invitations, we activate powerful, unlikely combinations—curiosity with persistence, empathy with assertiveness—that form resilient identities capable of enduring and transforming pressure.

I saw this recently in a coaching client named Jenna. After a career setback, she thought she needed to "armor up." But what actually helped her rebuild wasn't external toughness—it was the quiet blend of self-compassion and fierce discipline that carried her through. That unlikely pairing became her leadership superpower.

You don't have to lead a movement to live this way. Teachers whose curiosity, empathy, and dedication intertwine shape generations. Nurses, artists, parents, and entrepreneurs—anyone who allows their values to blend intentionally—can create a transformative impact.

Our values are always interacting. When you align them consciously, you don't just glow, you guide. You create a map for others to find their way home.

Embrace the Dance

Unleash your values like beams of Light—fluid, fearless, bending and refracting as they meet the sharp edges of life. In that intentional fusion, new strength is born. Resilience softens through compassion. Confidence deepens through humility. Joy expands through gratitude.

This is where untapped power awakens—not through grinding harder but by moving in harmony with who you are.

It isn't about forcing combinations or manufacturing balance. It's about discovering the natural choreography of your Core—like wind chimes catching sunLight, shifting and shimmering as the air around them changes.

Harmony isn't a static chord. It asks for your participation. It invites you to show up fully, to embrace both the clash and the congruence as your values find their evolving rhythm. Your strength isn't in eliminating the wobble. It's in the honest, beautiful work of staying steady through it.

This journey of harmonization never really ends. Each time you weave your values with intention, you create a Light that not only strengthens your Core but quietly guides others too.

Now that your inner rhythm is alive and steady, you're ready for the next movement—to let that Light reveal itself as leadership.

Being Enough

Letting values blend and deepen into new strength.

Finding worth in small, quiet victories.

Living as a constellation that gently guides others.

Chapter 14

Reveal

The Light Was Never Gone

The Remembering

At the start of each day, my dog and I step out into the desert darkness just before dawn. The air is crisp and still, holding its breath for what's about to unfold. We walk the same path each day, yet no two dawns are ever alike. Sometimes a family of deer pauses their grazing to watch us pass, their ears twitching in the growing glow. Other times, geese arrow overhead, their calls echoing across the quiet landscape. There are days when I use my cane or walker. Other days, I can balance on my own. Either way, we keep moving. Together. Waiting for the sky to change.

It starts subtly, a softening of the darkness, a hint of color at the horizon. Then, as if someone is slowly turning up nature's dimmer switch, the world awakens in layers. The first rays catch the highest clouds, painting them in brilliant oranges and pinks. These colors deepen and spread, like watercolors bleeding across wet paper. Below, the brown mountains wait their turn, quiet sentinels in the growing Light.

And then it happens. When the sun finally crests the horizon, those seemingly plain brown ridges begin to glow from within. Suddenly, their valleys and edges reveal shades I never knew existed—amber, copper, sienna, gold. What had looked flat moments ago now shimmers with depth. Birds rise on the morning winds, their wings catching the shimmer as they spiral upward.

Every day, it stuns me. Because the mountains don't become something new when the Light hits them. They don't stretch, shift, or suddenly evolve. They stay exactly what they are. What changes is how we see them. What was hidden becomes known. What looked plain begins to radiate. It's not transformation by force—it's illumination by presence.

This isn't just poetic. In physics, we call this albedo, an object's ability to reflect Light. The mountain doesn't create its own glow; it reveals it when Light strikes at the right angle. We're the same. We don't manufacture our brilliance. We remember how to reflect it.

The Reflection

You do not catch the light, you become the surface that reflects it.

Our essence—our Core Light—never disappeared. It's like a familiar song you haven't heard in years; the melody resurfaces, and with it, everything you thought you'd forgotten. Your values work like that too. They don't vanish. They wait, just under the surface, for a new chorus to begin. But some days, like those mountains, you sit under a shadow. On other days, a shift in perspective, grace, or season allows that same steady truth to shine through in new ways. On hazy days, your values might glow soft and warm. On clear days, they might shine sharp with conviction. And sometimes, when storms part just right, they pierce through with clarity you never expected.

The mountain doesn't have to chase the sun to matter. And neither do you.

This is the truth I carry within me now. Sometimes, I need help to move. Some days, I walk freely. But on all days, my worth is not in question. Not because of what I do, but because of what I am and always have been.

I remember one morning when I was already behind schedule, fumbling to start a Zoom workshop I was supposed to lead. My hands wouldn't cooperate with the keyboard, and my thoughts felt like scattered puzzle pieces. My body was having one of those days—tight, unpredictable, and uncooperative.

The old version of me would've panicked. I would've pushed harder, masked the struggle, and performed through the pain with a polished smile. But this version of me paused. I took a slow breath. Let the silence stretch. And entered the call. Not as the flawless leader I used to think I had to be, but as a human being doing her best.

The class unfolded in real time—messy, beautiful, and raw. I taught imperfectly. I lost my words. I paused often to catch the breath my muscles kept restricting. My voice trembled once or twice, but I kept showing up, letting gratitude spill out where control used to be.

Halfway through, a little blue Zoom hand appeared on the screen. A woman unmuted herself and said softly, "Thank you for being human. It's so good to see someone running their life through struggle, not around it."

Her words landed deep, like a chord that kept resonating long after the sound faded.

That moment reminded me: Light doesn't have to be perfect to shine. It wasn't polish that connected us that day. It was presence. That was Light—refracted through real life.

Your Light Revealed

This hasn't been a journey of reinvention. It's been a return. A revealing. A remembering.

Like those desert mountains, you've held wonder within you all along—depths and dimensions waiting to be seen by a different angle of sun. Your values have not vanished.

Your brilliance has not left. It's simply waiting—like the ridges and folds of the canyon—to be witnessed in this new Light.

When you live from that place, something shifts. You don't just cope—you guide. You don't just adapt—you align. You don't just glow—you become a wayfinder—a quiet Light that helps others find their own way through the dark.

You don't need to shine the brightest. You only need to shine from where you are.

And now, you're ready—not just to trust your Light, but to let it lead.

Some mornings, I still limp. Some mornings, I shine. But every morning, I step into the dark knowing the Light is coming. And so is the remembering.

As you move forward, you'll begin to see how that Light—steady and sacred—can take shape in the world around you.

Being Enough

Trusting that your light is constant even when hidden in shadow.

Showing up with honesty rather than perfection and letting that be connection.

Remembering that presence, not performance, is what illuminates others.

Realize

Part IV

Living Your Worth in Leadership
and Presence

Chapter 15

Connect

*When Your Values Connect with
Others, Your Impact Becomes a Legacy*

Shedding What's Not You

The hardest work is not discovery; it is alignment. I used to wear my roles like armor—the loyal employee, the high-achiever. But after the discipline of Subtraction. I knew alignment wasn't about putting more on; it was about the simple, courageous act of standing only in what was true. That's when your worth becomes something more than personal freedom: it becomes a legacy.

I didn't think of them as roles. They just felt like reality. Like expectations I was supposed to meet without asking who established them. But after my life forced me to pause, every time I tried that armor back on, it started to chafe. A subtle discomfort at first, like wearing a jacket that used to fit but now pinched in the shoulders and pulled at the seams. The more I tried to keep up, the more I disappeared.

This is where we begin. Not by doing more but by unlearning.

We learn early how to survive. We adapt. We achieve. We overfunction. We read the room and give it what it wants. But presence and performance aren't the same thing, and survival is not the same as shining. Even the brightest Lights burn out.

Lady Gaga, for all her extravagance, found herself hospitalized in 2010—exhausted, dehydrated, hollowed out by chasing what the industry wanted. I remember reading about it and thinking, Oh. Even her... Her pivot didn't begin with a costume. It began with a collapse. She wasn't doing less to disappear. She was doing less of what wasn't her, and in that choice, she began to shine in a way that could last.

Steve Jobs too—his obsession with beauty, story, and simplicity didn't fit the numbers-driven mold of the existing corporate container. He got pushed out. But when he came back, he didn't apologize. He refined his vision until the world finally caught up. His return was an act of aggressive Subtraction.

These high-profile pivots prove the point: you cannot be aligned while still wearing what society, family, or your past demand. It's a fundamental refusal. For me, that refusal didn't blaze or rage; it just refused quietly. I went home and wrote a story. Not for anyone. Just because I had to. I snuck spark into the sterile. I slipped color into the gray. It wasn't rebellion. It was remembrance.

And the more I honored my Core, the more others lit up. My clients. My students. Even strangers. They didn't need my effort. They needed my essence. My refusal to be less made room for others to be more. This is the quantum leap: from borrowed Light to embodied truth.

The Gravitational Legacy

There's a kind of power that doesn't come from performance. It doesn't dazzle. It doesn't demand. It just shows up—and stays.

I first felt it while volunteering at a historic site in Nauvoo, Illinois. My task was simple: greet visitors and share the stories of those early settlers. Their hardships. Their courage. Their quiet, steadfast lives.

But beneath the surface of those tales, I began to sense something more. Their strength wasn't measured in what they built but in what they believed. It was alignment, an unshakable inner compass tethered to something greater than circumstance. They didn't rely on certainty; they relied on connection. A fierce, quiet faith that held them upright when the world tilted.

Day after day, I told those stories—of women who crossed rivers with frozen dress hems, of men who built brick by trembling brick. I spoke to the visitors into the wind and watched people listen, nod, and then drift away. I never knew if the words lingered. Never knew if anything I said reached past the moment.

And yet, every time I spoke, I hoped—hoped that in their own unseen battles someone might find a bit of strength in the remembering.

That not-knowing began to weigh on me.

One evening, after a long shift, I confided in my site director, Sam Park, that it was starting to feel like speaking into the void.

Sam was a gregarious giant of a man—warm, booming, often smiling—an energy deeply rooted to those around him. He ran the site like a conductor: his direction was clear and powerful.

He paused. He looked me square in the eye. "You'll never know the impact you make." The words hung there, heavy, honest, and still. Sam didn't explain. He didn't need to. He simply took a step and went back to his work, leaving the silence to do its own kind of teaching.

Sam understood a truth I was still learning: that impact isn't a performance—it's a presence.

You don't have to witness the ripple to know the stone was thrown.

This phenomenon is rooted in what Dr. Kenneth Gergen calls relational being—the idea that our identity and meaning are continuously co-created through resonance. When you are deeply aligned, your presence naturally shapes others—not by pressure, but by frequency. Dr. Barbara Fredrickson's broaden-and-build theory confirms this. Your positive alignment expands the mindsets of those around you, building their lasting personal resources.

This is quiet impact, resonance over reach. The kind that guides others home to themselves simply because you're home in yourself.

The Constellation Effect

But this kind of Light never stops with us. When we live from our Core, our Light doesn't just shine, it aligns. And aligned Light can guide.

I saw this transformation unfold with my client, Crystal, the music teacher.

When she finally decided to do less of what was expected and do more of what felt true, the results were exponential.

"It's like... each person's Light strengthens the others."

"That's the Constellation Effect," I told her. "It's what happens when you live from your authentic values. You model possibility, not just productivity. And that has a multiplying impact."

This mirrors what Malcolm Gladwell describes as the tipping point—the moment when small, intentional actions accumulate and catalyze broad cultural shifts. A single aligned person can spark momentum that spreads and reshapes the collective.

We've seen it across history. The civil rights movement wasn't just Martin Luther King; it was a pattern of brave stars—marching, singing, sitting, rising. Your Light, aligned with others, becomes more than guidance. It becomes the gravitational legacy.

The Constellation Effect

Your light was never meant to shine alone. It was meant to belong to a constellation.

And in our own lives, it looks like this: the colleague whose quiet values energize the entire room, the family that shifts when one person chooses to speak their truth, the business that pivots because someone says, "This doesn't feel aligned."

Mapping Your Constellation

If you're wondering how to begin—how to live in alignment, how to become the kind of Light that guides—don't start with a checklist. Start with a return. Not a reinvention but a remembering.

Discover not how to shine brighter but how to shine truer.

Let these questions guide you home.

Name your Core Values. What truths have followed you, even when everything else fell away?

Notice your impact. When do others Light up around you without you trying?

Play with alignment. What happens when you lead with your Core Values?

Ask better questions. Where are you performing? Where are you present?

Reconnect. Who else shares your Light and what might happen if you let yourselves reflect each other?

The stars that guide us today have been shining for centuries—held in place by gravity and story, by memory and pattern. So have you.

You don't need to shine the brightest. You just need to be aligned.

You don't need to earn your Light—you only need to return to it. And in that alignment, your quiet radiance will travel farther than you can imagine. Do less. Shine farther. Align. And let the sky remember your name.

Being Enough

Shedding roles that no longer fit and choosing presence instead.

Trusting that quiet, aligned light leaves a deeper imprint than noise.

Living your truth so fully that it awakens light in others.

Chapter 16

Flow

Your Truest Rhythm Carries Your Purpose

Flow State Reflection

It started with a clock. I glanced up after a conversation and realized forty minutes had passed effortlessly. No timer. No notes. Just me, a whiteboard, and a small circle of people leaning in, nodding, and scribbling furiously.

The funny thing? It wasn't what I had scheduled. I was supposed to be doing something "more productive" like answering emails or pushing through reports.

But somehow, I'd gotten pulled into helping someone untangle a problem. And without even meaning to, I lit up. The fog cleared for them and for me. When we wrapped up, I felt more energized than when I'd begun.

Which didn't make sense. Not by the rules I'd been living under, anyway.

Was this moment just a fluke or a clue? Could I trust what felt good, even if it didn't look impressive on paper?

That's when I first realized: flow isn't just a pleasant feeling. It's a signal, a moment of energetic alignment with who you truly are. As pioneering psychologist Mihaly Csikszentmihalyi describes in his extensive research, flow emerges during moments of optimal experience when our skill level and the challenge before us are in perfect balance, resulting in deep engagement and enjoyment. We become so engrossed in an activity that nothing else seems to matter, and time often appears to distort.

I started paying attention. Not just to my schedule, but to my energy. I kept a notebook nearby and jotted things down—when I felt drained, when I left a conversation buzzing or bruised.

The patterns didn't scream—they whispered. Quiet but consistent. I felt most alive when I was guiding, reflecting, and illuminating, rather than producing for the sake of proving.

That's when it clicked. Energy wasn't just a byproduct. It was a compass.

The moments when I lost track of time weren't accidents—they were breadcrumbs. Markers pointing me back to my Core. Not toward doing more, but toward doing what was mine.

Your natural frequency isn't something you have to force. You've felt it before—when you were fully present, quietly joyful, and unmistakably you. The more you follow that current, the less you'll need to shine brighter. You'll simply shine truer.

Before you optimize your schedule, observe your soul.

Think back—not to what looked successful, but to what felt like clarity. When was the last time you looked up and realized an hour had passed without noticing? When were you so immersed in something that the edges of your awareness softened, your shoulders loosened, the clock blurred, and for a moment, it felt like everything clicked?

That's your clue.

Flow isn't loud. It doesn't announce itself. It shows up in the quiet hum of alignment when what you're doing matches who you are.

Start there. Jot down the moments that felt like that. You don't need to label them or explain why they mattered. Just notice.

What were you doing when time slipped away?

What activities leave you feeling full, not just finished?

Is there a pattern hiding in plain sight, something about guiding others, making meaning, solving puzzles, or telling the truth?

These aren't coincidences. They're coordinates. Follow the energy. It's already telling you where you shine.

But sometimes, what energizes us doesn't show up right away. I learned this the hard way—on a day when everything was perfectly arranged for flow, and yet...nothing flowed.

Finding Flow Through Discomfort

I remember sitting at my desk late one Thursday, blinking at my screen, trying to summon the spark I was supposed to feel.

I had cleared my calendar. Made time to "follow my flow." Everything was set up just right—hot tea, a color-coded to-do list, even a playlist that promised productivity.

But I felt nothing. No inspiration. No momentum. Just resistance.

This was supposed to be the experiment. The moment I'd pinpoint my purpose by tracking my energy.

I was doing everything right. But instead of feeling lit up, I felt dull and heavy.

So, I tried harder, forced myself to focus, rearranged tasks, and jumped from one half-finished idea to the next.

By the end of the day, I was more drained than when I'd started.

That was the first time I realized: flow doesn't show up on command. And maybe—just maybe—I was looking in the wrong place.

I started to pay attention—not to what I wanted to feel aligned with, but to what actually energized me.

And what I noticed shocked me.

The moments that left me glowing weren't in the places I'd expected. They weren't in my "official" work slots. They weren't on a content plan or project tracker.

They were in the unplanned moments—when I stayed late on a Zoom call helping someone untangle an idea, or when I paused mid-conversation and said, "Wait, let's try this," and their eyes lit up.

That's when I felt something click. A kind of clarity I couldn't manufacture, only follow.

It hit me slowly. My flow didn't come from creating systems or checking boxes. It came from illuminating paths. Whether I was teaching a group of entrepreneurs or guiding someone through a moment of self-doubt, I felt most alive when I helped others see—see options, see patterns, and see themselves.This sense of vitality, alignment, and deep engagement is precisely what psychologists Edward Deci and Richard Ryan describe in their self-determination theory. They propose that when our actions align with our innate psychological needs for autonomy (act-ing from choice), competence (feeling effective), and relatedness (connecting with others), we experience greater well-being, motivation, and a profound sense of purpose.

When people use this type of engagement, they not only solve problems but remember who they were in the process of doing so.

And I wasn't just energized. I was anchored.

The disappointment I'd felt before—of not finding my flow where I was "supposed to"—turned out to be a gift. A red flag waving me away from misalignment.

What I thought was failure was actually friction, guiding me toward something truer.

Discomfort became the invitation.

And in letting go of what didn't resonate, I began to do less...and shine farther.

The Impact Inventory

Sometimes your gifts are easiest to see through someone else's eyes—if you know how to listen.

There's a strange vulnerability in asking people how they see you. Sometimes the answers feel clear and true. Other times, they land sideways. Not wrong exactly. Just vague. Off-key.

I recall trying this once, gathering feedback about my presence, hoping it would guide me toward my Core essence. I wanted clarity, direction, something concrete.

What came back were words like "inspiring," "positive," and "such a Light."

Beautiful words. But they felt more like compliments than clues.

That's where the discomfort began. Not because the words were empty, but because I couldn't see how they connected to who I really was. They sounded like someone I was trying to be, not the someone I actually felt myself to be.

It made me wonder.

What do people really mean when they say "inspiring"?

Is that about me or about how they feel in my presence?

Am I listening to reflect or to be reassured?

When we're trying to live in alignment, it's tempting to reach outside ourselves for confirmation. We want others to echo something solid back to us. Something we can hold.

But over time, I learned to listen differently.

Instead of pushing for specific answers, I started listening for patterns. I paid attention to the moments when people lit up in conversation. The times they said, "That helped," or "You just made something click."

The language was still soft, but the impact felt real.

I wasn't being praised—I was being witnessed.

And that was the shift: realizing that feedback isn't always about performance. Sometimes it's about presence, what happens in the room when you're aligned.

When people say you're "positive," they may be naming your capacity to reflect possibility in hard places. When they say "inspiring," they may be referring to your quiet courage in keeping up the good work.

These aren't labels to chase. They're reflections of your Light. They don't define you; they help you remember what's already true.

The Energy Audit

Before you redesign your work, study your wiring.

There's a quiet kind of truth that reveals itself in the patterns we usually overlook.

For one week, try this. Don't change your schedule. Just pay attention to how it feels.

Before, during, and after each activity pause and ask these questions.

Does my body lean in or brace?

Do I leave this moment charged or foggy?

Does this align with who I am or is it just a box to check?

Noticing isn't always comfortable. Sometimes what we discover is inconvenient.

I assumed the moments that would energize me were the ones I had built my life around—teaching, leading, checking things off a long, color-coded list.

But when I started paying closer attention, the truth was harder to ignore.

Some things I thought should feel good...didn't.

I kept trying to explain the fatigue away, blaming it on deadlines, distractions, or not getting enough sleep. But underneath all that, I was resisting something deeper.

What I thought was burnout turned out to be misalignment.

This exercise didn't just show me what I liked or disliked. It revealed the places I had slowly shifted out of sync with myself. I had picked up tasks, roles, and rhythms that didn't reflect my natural frequency but fit someone else's idea of success.

And that's when the deeper work began.

Because once you see the misalignment, you can't unsee it. The question becomes: now that I know, what do I follow? And what do I release?

Honoring Your Natural Channels

Once you begin noticing the patterns—where your energy rises, where time expands, where your presence feels like enough—you may start to see something emerge.

Not a label. Not a job title. But a current. A way your Light wants to move.

These are your natural channels of expression, the ways you contribute without overreaching. The ways you resonate without trying.

It often feels easy, but not flashy. Effortless, but not accidental.

And still, it can be hard to trust them.

They don't always look like leadership. They may not feel big enough to make an impression. However, they are large enough to make a significant impact.

For me, this took time to accept. I wanted my strengths to be louder. More quantifiable. I thought if I could make my expression fit the mold—more measurable, more impressive—then it would matter more.

Flow

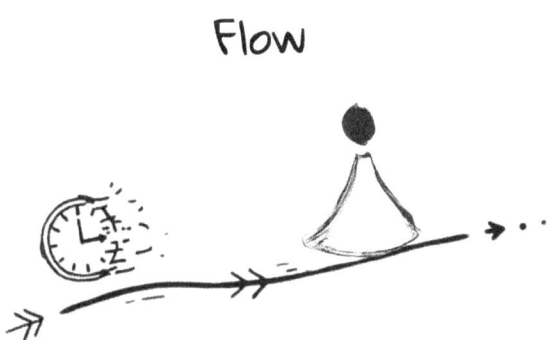

Stop watching the clock and start following your energy; that's where your truest self effortlessly moves.

However, that only served to distance me from what was already working.

Eventually, I stopped asking, "Is this enough?" and started asking, "Is this true?"

And when I followed what was true—again and again—it led me somewhere far more honest. More sustainable. More me.

Flow Alignment Practice: 3 Steps to Follow Your Frequency

You don't have to do more to shine brighter. You just have to notice where your Light already flows.

Track your energy. For one week, observe how you feel before, during, and after participating in various activities.

Ask:

When do I feel most alive and present?

What drains or dulls me, even if it "shouldn't"?

Keep a gentle log. No pressure, just awareness.

Name your flow moments. Reflect on moments when time seemed to stand still and your energy surged.

Ask:

What was I doing?

Who was I with?

What was the deeper pattern—guiding, solving, illuminating, or connecting? These are your natural channels. Honor what's true. Let the patterns shape your next steps.

Choose one task, one role, or one habit to let go of because it doesn't fit.

Choose one flow-aligned activity to prioritize, something that feels like you.

Small shifts toward resonance create space for real radiance.

You don't have to push to matter. You only have to pay attention. Flow isn't proof of success—it's a whisper from your soul. Follow it, and you'll find yourself.

Being Enough

Trusting the quiet pull of flow as a sign of alignment.

Letting discomfort guide you away from what no longer fits.

Following what energizes you even when it looks unimpressive.

Chapter 17

Redirect

Your Light Can Still Shine When the Path Shifts

Greatness, Redirected

I still remember the day I called Ann Marie at the Women's Business Center of Utah, asking if she needed any volunteers. Most mornings, I stared at the ceiling long after waking, my body still but my mind already racing. Not toward dreams or goals, but toward the ghost of something missing, like a door I once walked through but could no longer find.

A dull ache pulsed behind my ribs. It wasn't pain. It was emptiness, like I'd misplaced a vital piece of my soul and couldn't recall where.

A quiet longing lived under my skin, a sense that I was fading and I desperately needed something to tether me to who I still was.

Not for a job.

Not for a title.

Just something that felt real.

I was sitting on the floor of my bedroom, legs tucked unevenly beneath me, the carpet rough and flattened in patches where I'd paced that morning, my back pressed against the wall for support I didn't realize I needed.

The drywall felt cold through my shirt. Above me, a chipped piece of board caught the edge of the sunLight leaking through the blinds, casting thin gray stripes across the floor.

My laptop sat open at my side, humming faintly, its screen glowing with a half-written search—something about remote teaching jobs—but the cursor blinked like it was waiting on someone I couldn't quite be.

My hand trembled as I picked up my phone. My thumb hovered over Ann Marie's name, my heart thudding so loudly it pulsed in my ears—a trembling, silent plea for rescue.

But it wasn't small. It was a flicker of the me I feared I'd lost.

There was no plan, just the weight of silence I couldn't carry anymore.

She picked up right away. "Leisa, hi!" Just her voice was a ray of sunshine in my lost soul.

"I need something to do," I said.

"We're always looking for volunteers. If you want to do some outreach..."

So I did.

The first time I joined, I kept my mic and camera off—just a quiet square on the edge of someone else's story. But as I listened to an overwhelmed entrepreneur unravel her ideas, something stirred. Without thinking, I jotted down a few notes: a clearer way to explain her pitch, a better structure for her messaging.

It felt like teaching again but freer. Deeper. Like helping someone find their own logic in the chaos.

One session turned into three. Then into helping draft follow-up emails. Then into leading a few calls myself.

Volunteering turned into a small contract, a handful of hours a week. Enough to feel like I mattered. Enough to remember that: I hadn't vanished—I'd simply taken a different shape.

And eventually, that became a job. Not just work but a place I belonged. A place where I wasn't defined by what I couldn't do anymore but by what I still could.

I no longer needed to project my voice across a classroom or stand for hours. What I offered was presence.

What I brought was clarity, structure, and compassion, the ability to Light a path forward, even if I was still finding my own.

In losing the structure I'd once clung to, I found something softer. Wiser. Still powerful. I hadn't disappeared. I'd just shifted constellations.

This journey of finding deep meaning and purpose amidst profound life changes echoes the insights of Viktor Frankl, who taught that even in the most challenging circumstances, we retain the freedom to choose our attitude and find meaning in our unique response to life.

Core Values, Re-Expressed

Week by week, client by client, the pieces began to fall into place.

One Tuesday morning, I met with Jamila, a costume designer with a dream of opening her own shop. As she shared her vision, her voice trembled—part excitement, part fear.

I asked if she'd play a little game. She laughed, then began describing her work: the fabrics, the fit, the challenge of creating plus-sized costumes that actually flattered.

I stopped her gently. "No," I said. "What's the part you love, the part that fills your soul when you see someone in your designs?"

Her eyes welled up. "It's the confidence," she whispered. "The power they radiate when they put on something made just for them."

I smiled. "That's it. That's your foundation. That's what will set you apart. Now, let's start your business plan."

The creativity I'd once poured into lesson plans was now shaping blueprints for real-world dreams.

Another afternoon, Eliza stared at me through the computer screen, a woman who had spent years holding everyone else's world together while quietly setting aside her own. Her planner was full of other people's dreams. Now, for the first time, she was daring to build something of her own.

As she spoke, her words tumbled over one another, hope colliding with hesitation. Every idea she offered came wrapped in a disclaimer: "I'm not sure... Maybe it's silly... Who am I to think I could do that?" Her confidence flickered like a candle in a draft.

I listened—really listened—to the exhaustion beneath her careful optimism. Then I leaned forward and said softly, "What if your strength isn't in doing everything for others but in leading by showing what's possible?"

She went still. For a moment, the room was quiet except for the hum of the heater. Then she exhaled—a long, trembling release—and her shoulders dropped.

"No one's ever said that to me before," she whispered.

Something shifted in her eyes then. Not a blaze yet, but an ember that could kindle one.

This process of helping others reframe their experiences is central to narrative therapy, which emphasizes that by externalizing problems and re-authoring our life stories, we can open up new possibilities and reclaim agency.

Patience, once offered to six-year-olds learning to read, now steadied grown women learning to believe.

And over and over again, I witnessed the same transformation. Doubt giving way to courage. Fog giving way to clarity.

Each time, I saw their Light, and in uncovering theirs, I rediscovered mine.

This wasn't adaptation. It was alignment. I wasn't compromising. I was becoming more myself than ever.

Every breakthrough, every breath held in uncertainty, every glimmer of belief reflected back in their eyes—it was starLight. The same starLight I thought I'd lost.

It turns out that it had never gone out. It had just found a new sky to shine.

Full-Circle Moments

Each client became a mirror, reminding me that my purpose wasn't tied to a podium. It was in my presence. And even though the pace was slower, the depth was greater.

Another day, I found myself sharing encouragement with a fellow mom who had just received her own chronic illness diagnosis. No stage. No script. Just two women on a park bench, trading stories and breath.

It wasn't what I would've called leadership before, but it was.

It was quiet
influence.
Grounded hope.
A ripple.

This isn't just my story. Beethoven, when robbed of his hearing, composed from memory, creating the Ninth Symphony in total silence. Monet, whose cataracts blurred his vision, reimagined beauty with broad brushstrokes and bolder color.

They didn't just persist. They pivoted. Their genius adapted. Their essence evolved. They were forced to do less than their old forms, but their unwavering Core Light led them to shine farther in new, profound ways. Sometimes our greatest works are born not in spite of limitations but through them.

The science supports this redirection.

Resilience is dynamic, not fixed. Research highLights that resilience is a dynamic process involving adaptive responses to adversity and the cultivation of specific coping mechanisms.

Neuroplasticity is the brain's quiet miracle, its ability to adapt, reroute, and rediscover itself in response to change. It's the biological proof that growth is always possible, that even when life rewrites the map, we can still find new ways to move, to function, and to express who we are becoming.

Core Values, when expressed through new channels, activate new meaning networks and restore direction.

Even on gray mornings, our Light does not vanish. It pivots. It finds a new angle. A new reflection. A new direction in which to glow.

Same Star, New Constellations

Your worth—like starLight— doesn't fade when it bends. It refracts. It finds new constellations. And it keeps shining.

Whether you're navigating a chronic illness, a career shift, or simply a new chapter in life, your essence remains true.

You are not starting over. You are being redirected into a more aligned expression of who you've always been.

Pivot

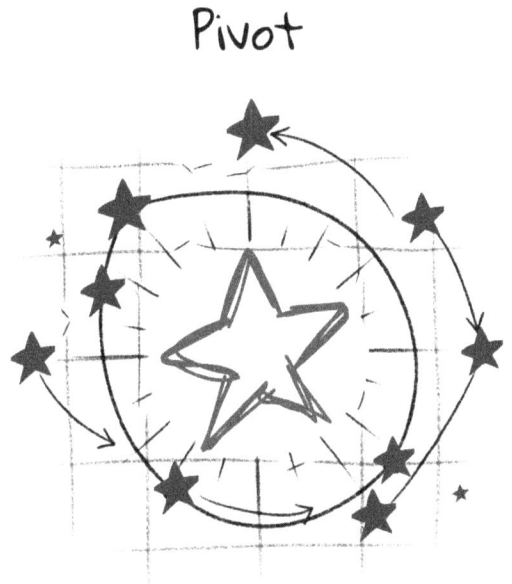

Greatness isn't found in the path you planned—it's revealed in the courage to shine from the one you were given.

Ask:

What Core Values have always guided me, no matter the role?

How might those values find new expression in this season?

Where could my strengths offer unexpected value?

What outdated version of success might I still be mourning?

What new constellation of meaning is ready to emerge?

Your Core Light
can guide any path
you choose to walk.

And when you trust that Light, you don't just navigate—you become a map for others.

So when life invites you to pivot, don't ask: "Who am I now?" Ask: "Where else can my Light shine, undimmed, just differently directed?"

Let yourself bend. Let yourself shift. Let yourself be reformed—not by fear, but by love, by purpose, and by presence.

Because when the old road ends, it doesn't mean the journey is over. It means it's time to walk by starLight.

Trust your Light. Pivot with purpose. And let each new constellation reveal the brilliance that's always been yours.

Being Enough

Trusting that your worth has not disappeared but is
finding new forms.

Letting core values re-express themselves as life changes.

Pivoting with purpose knowing redirection is not loss.

Chapter 18

Focus

Fewer Things, Deeper Impact.

One Word, One Spark

If redirection was learning to bend my Light, this was where I began to aim it.

The gray, overcast morning mirrored the weight I carried inside. Each step beside my dog felt like walking through fog, MS clinging to me like a sodden coat I couldn't shrug off. I wasn't even far from home, but the exhaustion hollowed me out.

My legs faltered. My breath grew shallow. The sidewalk blurred as I sank onto the cold, wet cement—defeated. My dog bounced beside me, tail wagging, unaware that we were now living in two entirely different realities: hers full of energy, mine stripped bare.

I sat there, aching and humiliated, wondering: was this it? Was this who I had become?

I couldn't push forward. I couldn't go back. All I could do was sit in the in-between, stranded between the life I had and the one I no longer knew how to live.

Then, everything changed.

The clouds, thick and unmoving all morning, parted for just a breath. A single beam of sunLight broke through, cutting across the sky and landing, impossibly, right at my feet.

I didn't move. I just watched it. I let it warm the damp concrete beneath me. I let it remind me that even in collapse, Light can still arrive. It only lasted a moment, but it was enough.

Sitting on the ground, waiting for my husband to come get me, I began to understand something profound.

I hadn't lost my ability to shine. I was being asked to shine differently. This wasn't about giving up; it was about surrendering control over the how, to allow a deeper, truer what to emerge.

I had forgotten that, even when obscured, Light finds a way. MS was dimming my ability to do, yes, but it hadn't extinguished my being. My Light wasn't gone. It was narrowing. Honing. Preparing for precision. And in that quiet realization, something shifted.

I hadn't lost everything. I hadn't lost me.

Light Narrows, Stars Sharpen

In that quiet recalibration, I found myself returning again and again to a single image.

Imagine an old Lighthouse guiding ships through the dark. It doesn't try to illuminate the entire ocean—it casts a focused beam right where it's needed most. That precise beam, not a broader effort, is what turns danger into safety.

It doesn't try to do everything. It does the essential thing with intention.

This image of directional Light stayed with me. It wasn't just a metaphor for efficiency; it became a matter of survival. I had to learn that reducing my output didn't mean dimming my purpose.

That principle of focused effort reminded me of a surprising example: the story of Sir Dave Brailsford and British Cycling. He believed greatness lived in the tiniest of tweaks—a better night's sleep, a millimeter adjustment on the seat, a more breathable fabric. Rather than overhauling everything, he improved what already existed by just 1%—over and over again.

The result? One hundred seventy-eight world championships, sixty-six Olympic and Paralympic golds, and five Tour de France wins.

Their brilliance didn't come from doing more. It came from focusing better.

That, to me, is the essence of focus, the art of directional Light. Channeling our values, energy, and gifts into a precise beam of purpose—steady, deliberate, and deeply impactful.

Finding My Beam

After my MS diagnosis, I no longer had long, boundless days. I had to reimagine how I lived, worked, and led. It was no longer about maximizing hours; it was about maximizing impact within dwindling capacity.

I started designing my day around my highest energy windows, those golden hours when my mind felt clear and my body was still capable of following.

Directional Light

It's not about dimming your light;
it's about directing it.

Your highest energy window is the time of day when you feel most alive—physically, mentally, or emotionally. To find yours, ask:

When do I feel most clearheaded or most emotionally grounded?

What time of day do I most often get into flow?

What drains me fastest, and what restores me quickest?

Once you identify it, protect it as if it were a sacred appointment. Use it not for tasks but for impact.

Surprisingly, my impact increased. Clients began telling me, "That one focused hour with you was more useful than entire retreats."

I wasn't doing more. I was doing what mattered, more intentionally.

I was doing less, but the focused quality of my being in those hours helped others shine even brighter.

This shift taught me something powerful. Like a single well-placed lamp in a dark room, your energy can reveal what's most important when focused with care.

The Psychology of Precision

Positive psychology backs this up. Dr. Barbara Fredrickson's broaden-and-build theory shows that positive emotions don't flourish in chaos. They grow best in intentional, emotionally attuned environments.

Likewise, neuroscience tells us that focused attention forms stronger neural connections, improves learning, and enhances emotional regulation. When we stop scattering our energy, our brilliance deepens.

You don't have
to shine everywhere.
You just have
to shine true.

Anne Sullivan understood this. She didn't try to teach Helen Keller the entire world in a day. She taught her the sign for water. Over and over again. That one focused moment cracked open an entire language.

That same spark appears across various disciplines, including education, psychology, and leadership. MIT's Social Impact Lab refers to these as catalyst moments—a beam of effort, in the right place at the right time, that ignites something bigger.

I've seen it in coaching calls, whispered prayers, and shared stories online. Focused presence becomes a map for someone else. A Lighthouse waiting to be ignited.

While researching stories of adaptive resilience, I met Michelle, a former Radio City Rockette. MS ended her dancing career. For a while, she believed it ended her purpose too.

But instead of turning off the Light, she narrowed the beam.

She mentored. She choreographed. She reminded young dancers that grace is not about perfection; it's about presence.

"I thought MS would close the curtain," she told me. "Instead, it gave me a bigger stage."

Michelle's directional Light didn't fade—it focused.

Her impact deepened. Her roots grew. Her ripple widened.

Her story reflects what scientists call adaptive resilience, not bouncing back to old form but bending toward a new expression of the same Core self.

Michelle's new Light created: stronger mentoring relationships, expanded community impact, deeper personal fulfillment.

She didn't do more. She did what mattered most, with clarity and intention.

Instead of clinging to a past version of success, she redirected her energy toward building something rooted and lasting.

You don't have to be an Olympic coach or a world-class dancer. Focused presence—offered exactly where you are—can ripple just as far.

This is the professional turning point for so many of us. Stop doing everything. Start directing your energy toward what truly matters.

Your Beam of Impact

I stopped trying to flood every room with Light and started noticing where it was needed most. I wrote one heartfelt note instead of replying to every message. I listened—really listened—to a friend instead of filling silence with advice. I let my hands move slowly, stitching small things with care. And somehow, in doing less, the Light felt truer.

Not scattered. Not wasted. Just...homed in.

What I couldn't do no longer defined me. What I chose to give—thoughtfully, deliberately—became a quiet kind of leadership.

Not by striving but by shining, steady and sure, in the places that mattered most.

So pause. Recenter. Aim your Light with purpose. Don't worry about Lighting the whole sky. That's not your job.

Your job is to shine right where it matters most. Even one steady beam can become a map for someone else. One moment of focused presence can change everything.

Being Enough

Letting your light narrow into focus rather than scatter everywhere.

Honoring your highest energy by giving it where it matters most.

Trusting that one steady presence can ripple farther than striving.

Chapter 19

Witness

The Final Awakening: Your Value,
Unmeasured and Infinite

The Return

Five years had passed since I'd first lain flat beneath the humming magnet of the MRI machine—my hands shaking, the gown loose around me, my world spinning sideways. Five years since Dave, the hospital pharmacist, handed me a stack of printed papers explaining my diagnosis, before gently reminding me, "life is good."

And on the anniversary, I found myself back in that same hospital, not for a scan but for the slow drip of medicine meant to hold me steady. My body hadn't improved, but I had. I wasn't here searching for answers this time. I had come to stay in rhythm with what I already knew.

Healing, I had learned, wasn't always forward. Sometimes it was deeper.

And then, just like the first time, Dave appeared.

Still in his button-up shirt with that easy calm. The same man who had offered me warmth when everything felt like it was falling. And just as he did before, he pulled up a chair. "They've got a new MRI machine," he said with a dry chuckle. "My scans show lesions in the hundreds now."

Hundreds

My breath caught. I had spent years counting mine in double digits—twenties, maybe. That number had loomed like a shadow. But next to his, mine suddenly felt slight. Feathery. Insignificant.

"They think it's just clearer imaging," he added, as if it mattered. But we both knew that probably wasn't the case. His MS was progressing. The medication that had once kept him from getting worse was losing its grip. He would need to change courses. And there were no promises that the next one would work.

But there he sat—smiling. Unafraid to let the tears fill his eyes. Not because he wasn't afraid, but because he had made peace with presence. Not in denial, and not in false optimism either. Just fully present.

You Were Never Gone

It wasn't a reinvention; it was a return. The true self doesn't wait to be fixed, it waits to be seen.

His profound peace in the face of progressive illness powerfully illustrates Viktor Frankl's Core tenet: that while we cannot always control our circumstances, we always retain the freedom to choose our attitude and find meaning in our response to life. This meaning is cultivated not only through action but through the attitude we take toward unavoidable suffering.

It also reflects what Tedeschi and Calhoun describe as posttraumatic growth—a transformation that doesn't erase hardship but reveals strength, perspective, and a deeper sense of purpose through it.

Dave spoke of changes. Letting go of projects. Reworking his responsibilities. Adjusting how he served in his church. But he didn't sound like someone diminishing. He sounded like someone distilling. Not someone shrinking but someone refining.

I watched as nurses walked past and waved in greeting. Not concerned about how hard he worked, but grateful for the Light he gave.

"It's our five-year anniversary," I said, half-laughing, phone in hand. "We should get a picture." He leaned in, his shoulders relaxed. And as I snapped the photo, I saw it, etched in the creases at the corner of his eyes. That rare kind of brilliance. The kind that doesn't rise from effort but from essence. The kind that doesn't shout. It simply stays.

This enduring, quiet influence is a hallmark of what Kenneth Gergen describes as relational being, where our very identity and impact are co-created within our connections with others. Dave's authentic presence, unburdened by external performance, allows his essence to resonate deeply simply by being a fully attuned, aligned self.

Later, I stared at that photo, and something stirred inside me.

Not envy. Not pity. Recognition. Of something older than ambition.

He was no longer trying to outpace his illness. And he wasn't trying to earn his place. He was already there—anchored in something deeper than productivity, deeper than roles, deeper than the body that once moved faster.

Sociologist Kathy Charmaz wrote about how illness disrupts not just the body, but the self and how healing often comes not through a cure but through reshaping one's identity in Light of limitation. That was Dave. He hadn't just adapted his schedule. He had realigned his selfhood. Everything he had shed—his stamina, his sharp edge of control—had made more room for his essence to shine through. This was not deterioration. This was a revelation.

The Realignment

I thought: what if this is the leap we never knew we needed?

Not from broken
to whole. Not
from sick to
cured. But from
proving to being.

That day, I didn't see a man deteriorating. I saw a man distilled.

This wasn't resilience in the way we usually mean it. It wasn't bouncing back. It was bending toward brilliance.

Adaptive. Anchored. Alive.

A Light that had burned away everything false until only the truth remained.

A quiet kind of leadership. The kind that doesn't need a stage. The kind that glows through disruption, not in spite of it. That day, I witnessed the real quantum leap.

Not from failure to success. But from striving to stillness. From performance to presence.

From chasing impact to embodying it. The kind of shift that doesn't demand more. It invites you to do less of what is no longer true. And in doing so shine further than you ever imagined.

Even in seasons of loss, your essence remains. Even in the dimmest hours, your Light remembers how to burn.

This is not reinvention. This is realignment.

You were never gone. You were always becoming.

Let that become your truth. You are not waiting to be fixed. You are waiting to be seen.

And when the noise falls away—when the proving ends—what remains isn't diminished.

It's revealed.

It's radiant.

It's you.

Being Enough

Letting go of proving and allowing presence its quiet
brilliance.

Distilling who you are until what remains is essence.

Trusting that even loss can reveal light.

Chapter 20

Lead

Your Essence Was Never Gone—Only Waiting to Be Lived Again

Light Realized

It began with starLight. A quiet night, a quiet ache. And a single question: could what I had remembered in the dark become something others could carry in the Light?

After discovering the connection between worth and starLight that night, I began the slow, intricate work of translation—turning revelation into language, ache into architecture. There were days I felt like I was trying to bottle starLight or balance equations made of fire. But then I'd remember what it felt like to sit in the dark and suddenly be seen—not changed, but remembered.

This wasn't a theory I was building. It was a truth I was tracing—backward, inward, home.

Human worth, I realized, behaves like Light itself, constant at its Core, adaptive in its expression. We are not fixed points. We are living patterns. Constellations that shift, stretch, and survive, even when one Light dims.

Now, the final truth remains. Could this idea survive the bright, harsh Lights of the outside world?

Illumination, Not Invention

The ballroom of the Hyatt in downtown D.C. shimmered beneath crystal chandeliers, the air thick with heat and the quiet hum of nerves. My name sat folded on a card in my lap: National Business Advisor of the Year Nominee. I commanded myself to breathe, but adrenaline had already overridden my body's software.

When they began calling the nominees, I rose with the others to take my place on stage, my cane tapping softly against the carpet, the sound a metronome counting out my courage. The Lights were blinding. The applause rolled like distant thunder.

I knew what was coming. The heat pressed against my skin, and the adrenaline sent my MS into high gear. My legs stiffened, turning to stone beneath the black jacket.

Two small stairs separated me from the stage, a distance that suddenly felt like a mountain range.

I took a breath, gripped the railing, and pulled myself upward—one deliberate, wrestling step at a time—straight into the arms of a beautiful woman in a floral dress. She took my arm without hesitation, her warmth steady and sure. Her touch was the quiet, human anchor I needed. You're safe here, her grip seemed to say. You belong here.

Cameras flashed. Heartbeats quickened.

And then they said my name: "Leisa Wallace, 2025 National Business Advisor of the Year."

For a moment, everything went still. The room blurred—the Lights, the applause, the thousand small faces I could no longer focus on. It was as if time itself had paused, holding its breath with me.

Applause broke like a wave, crashing through the stillness. My chest tightened; my throat caught fire. The woman beside me lifted the certificate for me to hold, her hands steady where mine trembled.

Somewhere behind the roar, I heard my own heartbeat. Not the frantic rhythm of hustle, but the steady, fragile drum of something I hadn't known I'd been waiting to hear. You made it. Not because you earned it—because you endured.

The president of the conference leaned in, her voice cutting gently through the noise. "Would you like to say something?"

From Divine Doing
to Diving Being

The pursuit of worth leaves you striving. The recognition of worth sets you free to be.

I turned toward the room, a sea of women who had dedicated their lives to helping others rise. And in that moment, it hit me—every sleepless night, every flare-up, every whispered prayer to remember who I was when the doing stopped.

Standing there, cane in hand, I knew: this was the moment everything I had written, wrestled, and rebuilt was meant to meet the world.

The words came like a memory finding their way home.

"We don't know what the future will bring," I began. "Our titles will shift. Our roles will change. But when we remember the Core of who we are—and help our clients remember who they are—we can pivot with purpose. We can evolve without losing ourselves. Because the work isn't to prove our value. It's to remember it and to help others do the same."

The room fell still—not silent, but sacred.

And as I stood there beneath the ballroom Lights—legs trembling, heart steady—I felt the full circle of it all. This was the Adaptive Light bending to the moment, fragile yet fierce. But the Core Light—the truth in my voice—was unshaken.

The girl who once believed she had to earn her value had become the woman who embodied it.

That night, I didn't just hold an award. I held proof that the message I had once whispered to myself in the dark had finally found its way into the Light. Because human worth, like starlight, cannot be boxed or broken. It pulses, it evolves, and above all, it endures.

The Final Charge

Your Light was never meant to be earned. It was made to be aimed, to be aligned, to reach.

You are not broken. You are a constellation—shifting shape, still shining. Your impact is not in your effort. It's in your essence.

The ones who shine brightest aren't untouched by struggle. They're the ones who remember their Light through difficulty—who choose alignment over applause, stillness over striving, essence over effort.

And now—your story begins.

It doesn't need your perfection. It only needs your permission.

It always begins in the quiet. When the noise fades and the to-do lists dissolve, you hear it—the faint hum beneath everything that's changed. That's the beginning of Remembering. You pause long enough to trace your own pulse, to feel the steady rhythm that never left. You begin to see that your worth was never something to be earned; it was the current carrying you all along. That's how the Worth Paradox breaks—not with effort, but with recognition.

Then comes Reclaiming. It isn't loud or defiant. It happens in the smallest acts of courage, the moment you finally say "no" when you mean no or when you let yourself rest before collapse. You learn that stillness isn't weakness; it's strength refined. The Subtraction begins here—the sacred, deliberate work of releasing everything that was never truly yours to carry.

And finally, you Realize. You stop trying to prove and start to embody. You speak your name with tenderness, letting it ring true in every room you enter. You lead not by striving but by shining. Your choices, your rhythm, your presence—they become your testimony. This is your Constellation Map, the truth that holds even when everything else shifts. It's a rhythm—a way of walking through the world that remembers what is constant, reclaims what is true, and lives from what was never lost.

One day, someone—standing in their own dark—will see your glow and remember their own.

That's how constellations are born. One Light remembering another.

Go gently.

Shine bravely.

And remember—you are already enough.

Being Enough

Remembering your worth is not earned but uncovered.

Living from alignment rather than applause.

Offering your light as illumination rather than proof.

Thank You

Books may have one name on the cover, but they're never written alone. This one was built with laughter, caffeine, grace, and a whole lot of people who refused to let me give up when the words got hard. You've each shaped this book in ways you may never realize, and I'm endlessly grateful.

To my beta reader, Jess — thank you for believing in this book from the very beginning and for catching the little things (and the big heart things) that made it shine brighter.

To my writing crew — Amber, Amy, Courtney, Kim, and Jess — I'll never forget our early Saturday mornings and quarterly retreats filled with too much laughter, a little frustration, and so much heart. We've dreamed, vented, brainstormed, and cheered each other through every chapter. You made the process feel like play. WT#B

To my editors — Catherine Lundardon, my book strategist; Rachelle Funk, my detail magician; and Sarah

Ward, my final proofing hero — Catherine, I'm convinced fate hand-delivered you to me to turn my pile of ideas into something real. Rachelle, thank you for catching all the things I missed (and never judging my comma choices). And Sarah, thank you for catching the tiny things and helping me land this book with grace.

And to my husband and kiddos — my rock, my support, my cooks, my therapists, and the best family in the universe — thank you for loving me through the chaos, cheering for every win, and reminding me to drink something other than Diet Dr Pepper. I love you for eternity (and then some).

References

Bandura, Albert. 1994. Social Learning Theory. Englewood Cliffs, NJ: Prentice-Hall.

Barrett, Lisa Feldman. 2017. How Emotions Are Made: The Secret Life of the Brain. Boston: Houghton Mifflin Harcourt.

Gladwell, Malcolm. 2000. The Tipping Point: How Little Things Can Make a Big Difference. Boston: Little, Brown.

Charmaz, Kathy. 1995. "The Body, Identity, and Self: Adapting to Impairment." The Sociological Quarterly 36, no. 4: 657–680.

Csikszentmihalyi, Mihaly. 1990. Flow: The Psychology of Optimal Experience. New York: Harper & Row.

Davidson, Richard J., and Sharon Begley. 2012. The Emotional Life of Your Brain: How Its Unique Patterns Affect the Way You Think, Feel, and Live—and How You Can Change Them. New York: Hudson Street Press.

Deci, Edward L., and Richard M. Ryan. 2000. "The 'What' and 'Why' of Goal Pursuits: Human Needs and the

Self-Determination of Behavior." Psychological Inquiry 11, no. 4: 227–268.

Doidge, Norman. 2007. The Brain That Changes Itself: Stories of Personal Triumph from the Frontiers of Brain Science. New York: Viking.

Dweck, Carol S. 2006. Mindset: The New Psychology of Success. New York: Random House.

European Space Agency. n.d. "How stars shine." ESA.int. Accessed April 20, 2024. _Exploration/Space_Science/How_stars_shine.

Frankl, Viktor E. 1984. Man's Search for Meaning. New York: Washington Square Press.

Fredrickson, Barbara L. 2009. Positivity: Top-Notch Research Reveals the 3-to-1 Ratio That Will Change Your Life. New York: Crown Archetype.

—. 2001. "The Role of Positive Emotions in Positive Psychology: The Broaden-and-Build Theory of Positive Emotions." American Psychologist 56, no. 3: 218–226.
.

Gergen, Kenneth J. 2009. Relational Being: Beyond Self and Community. Oxford: Oxford University Press.

House, John. 1986. Monet: Nature into Art. New Haven, CT: Yale University Press.

Heath, Chip, and Dan Heath. 2010. Switch: How to Change Things When Change Is Hard. New York: Broadway Books.

Kaler, James B. 1997. Stars and Their Spectra: An Introduction to the Spectral Sequence. Cambridge: Cambridge University Press.

Keller, Helen. 1903. The Story of My Life. New York: Doubleday, Page & Co.

Lakoff, George, and Mark Johnson. 2003. Metaphors We Live By. Chicago: University of Chicago Press.

Levine, Peter A. 2010. In an Unspoken Voice: How the Body Releases Trauma and Restores Goodness. Berkeley, CA: North Atlantic Books.

Muller, Jerry Z. 2018. The Tyranny of Metrics. Princeton, NJ: Princeton University Press.

Peterson, Christopher, and Martin E. P. Seligman. 2004. Character Strengths and Virtues: A Handbook and Classification. Oxford: Oxford University Press.

Ratey, John J. 2008. Spark: The Revolutionary New Science of Exercise and the Brain. New York: Little, Brown.

Ridpath, Ian. 2007. Star Tales: The Myths and Legends of the Constellations. Cambridge: Cambridge University Press.

Rogers, Carl R. 1961. On Becoming a Person: A Therapist's View of Psychotherapy. Boston: Houghton Mifflin.

Rushkoff, Douglas. 2013. Present Shock: When Everything Happens Now. New York: Penguin.

Southwick, Steven M., and Dennis S. Charney. 2012. Resilience: The Science of Mastering Life's Greatest Challenges. Cambridge: Cambridge University Press.

Swafford, Jan. 2014. Beethoven: Anguish and Triumph. New York: Houghton Mifflin Harcourt.

Tedeschi, Richard G., and Lawrence G. Calhoun. 2004. "Posttraumatic Growth: Conceptual Foundations and Empirical Evidence." Psychological Inquiry 15, no. 1: 1–18.

White, Michael, and David Epston. 1990. Narrative Means to Therapeutic Ends. New York: W. W. Norton & Company.

Created to Shine

A Companion to the Ultimate Act of Being Enough.

You've walked through the remembering. You've re-claimed what was buried beneath the noise. Now comes the realizing—the steady, beautiful work of letting your Light lead.

To help you carry this into daily practice, I created the Created to Shine Workbook—a companion guide to keep your alignment alive and embodied. Inside, you'll expand on the ideas and metaphors from this book, map your full Value Constellation, and uncover the strengths that have been quietly guiding you all along.

It's an invitation to live from your Core, to root deeper, shine brighter, and lead with unshakable clarity.

Visit AuthorLeisaWallace.com

(Your workbook awaits. Let your Light lead.)

Book Club

Part 1: Unravel

Chapters 1–5: Unravel, Collapse, See, Grieve, Question

These questions explore the beginning of the journey, the moments when life forces you to stop and a new sense of self begins to emerge.

1. When have you felt reduced to a number, a title, or a diagnosis, and what essential part of you got lost in that moment?

2. What unwanted labels or limiting definitions have been placed on you, and how have you quietly resisted or actively begun to redefine them?

3. What "planned version" of your life are you still holding onto, and what might change if you allowed yourself the space to grieve it fully?

Part 2: Remember

Chapters 6–9: Notice, Remember, Trust, Name

These questions focus on the process of re-remembering your Core worth and beginning to live from a place of presence, not performance.

1. In a world that equates worth with metrics, what part of you still believes you have to prove your value? What might shift if you trusted it was already there?

2. Think of a time when you sensed the truth of your worth before you could fully believe it. What helped you start to remember that truth?

3. If you peeled back every role and achievement, what single word or Core essence would rise to the surface? What qualities have remained steady in you, even when the metrics failed?

Part 3: Reclaim

Chapters 10–14: Wrestle, Subtract, Shape, Harmonize, Reveal

These questions explore how to actively reclaim your identity and choose how you express your Light in the world.

1. What inherent qualities have always burned quietly at your Core before roles or achievements gave them a name?

2. When have you felt most fully yourself—aligned, resonant, and deeply alive? What specific values or strengths were shining through you in that moment

3. When you consciously stop striving and simply "be," what forgotten parts of your Core begin to reappear and guide you?

Part 4: Realize

Chapters 15–20: Connect, Flow, Redirect, Focus, Witness, Lead

These questions help you apply the lessons of the book, translating inner alignment into outward impact and legacy.

1. Think of a time when your quiet presence made a difference in someone else's life, even if you didn't know it at the time. How might your Light already be guiding others?

2. Where in your life are you being invited to lead—not by doing more but by being more aligned? How might your essence be your greatest impact?

3. What would it mean to build a legacy rooted in presence, not performance?

About the Author

Leisa Wallace lives at the intersection of high-level strategy and radical grace. While she is the 2025 National Business Advisor of the Year, she knows firsthand that a title is not a soul—and it certainly won't carry you through real life.

After an MS diagnosis in 2019 brought her productivity-first lifestyle to a halt, Leisa began answering the question: *Who am I when the doing stops?* Today, she mentors from that hard-earned truth, proving that success doesn't have to cost you yourself.

Leisa lives in Utah's high desert with her husband, two children, and a lively menagerie of goats, cats, and dogs. She believes our greatest work isn't what we produce, but who we already are—messy, human, and already enough.

Connect with Leisa:

authorleisawallace.com | @chronically.thriving.leisa